"I am with you always."

- Jesus

The Joyful Catholic

Finding God's Love In Joy or Suffering

by
Frederick Hermann

Imprimatur #3412
The Joyful Catholic: Finding God's Love In Joy or Suffering

In accordance with Canon 827, permission to publish has been granted on October 24, 2012, by the Most Reverend Robert J. Carlson, Archbishop, Archdiocese of St. Louis. Permission to publish is an indication that nothing contrary to church teaching is contained in this work. It does not imply an endorsement of the opinions expressed in the publication; nor is any liability assumed by this permission.

Library of Congress Cataloging-in-Publication Data

Hermann, Frederick A.
        The Joyful Catholic: Finding God's Love In Joy or Suffering / Frederick Hermann

p. cm.
ISBN-13: 978-1482620931

ISBN-10: 1482620936
Religious life
        1. Spirituality
        2. Finding God
        3. Joy
        4. Grief
        5. Sadness
        6. Rejoice

Published by Frederick A. Hermann thru CreateSpace

Scripture taken from the NEW AMERICAN STANDARD BIBLE®,
Copyright © 1960,1962,1963,1968,1971,1972,1973,1975,1977,1995
by The Lockman Foundation. Used by permission.

Printed and bound in the
United States of America

Preface

Dear Reader,

If you are young or old, rich or poor, happy or sad, these stories will help you discover the amazing love of God.

Each story is like a parable containing pearls of wisdom. You may dive deep to retrieve these pearls, or you may find them near the surface, easily within your grasp.

Let them surprise you, like modern-day parables, as you discover the priceless gift of God's love hidden in each one.

They are meant to bring you peace, comfort and joy, even in the midst of sadness, grief or sorrow.

These reflections were originally syndicated to 40 Catholic newspapers and magazines reaching a potential audience of over four million people. People write me notes of thanks, and this makes me profoundly grateful.

I give thanks to my three sisters, Holly Hermann Gulick, Lyn Hermann Grace, and Mary Hermann Lemkemeier, who proofread these stories and infused them with their feminine genius.

Thanks especially to our Father, Son, and Holy Spirit.

Rick Hermann
St. Louis, MO

P.S. Books are best circulated – please give this one to a friend!

Where is God?

By Frederick Hermann

"Where is God?" you may say.
He often seems so far away.

"I've looked here, and there, and everywhere,
but I cannot find him anywhere!"

Ah, dear friend, be still and pray,
and catch a glimpse of God today.

Look very near and not afar,
Right there behind the cookie jar!

Look outside in trees and flowers;
see him exercising Divine powers?

Listen to your dearest friends;
Their words of love to you God sends.

Deep in your heart; now do you hear it?
That quiet voice is the Holy Spirit…

He's searching for you, to set you free,
Let him find you on bended knee.

Gently flowing at your side,
Rejoicing as your faithful Guide.

Embracing you from up above
With arms of everlasting love.

God is near indeed, you see:
Caressing all your needs, for free.

Give him all your earthly care;
Then you'll find him everywhere!

Table of Contents

HEALING

HOPING

LOVING

REJOICING

SEEKING

"Seek, and you will find."

- Jesus

† Seek and find the face of God

A little girl at school clutched her crayon tight as she scrawled and sketched with intense concentration.

Her teacher asked, "What are you drawing?"

The girl whispered, "It's a picture of God."

"Oh, dear," the teacher replied, "no one knows what God looks like."

Without hesitating, the girl declared, "They're about to find out."

If you are struggling to find God in your life, it helps to have the simple faith of a child.

"Seek my face," God asks us in Psalm 27. God wants us to find him. He eagerly runs to embrace us, like the father of the prodigal son.

Jesus found God by praying alone in the desert, and as a result, his face "shone like the sun".

We find God the same way, in prayer, and we have the sacraments to help us.

How do we know when we have seen God?

Moses' face became radiant. The disciples were filled with confidence and left their boats. Peter fell to his knees and asked forgiveness. Paul felt scales falling from his eyes.

We know one experience is common to all: an overwhelming sense of God's love and "peace which transcends understanding." (Phil. 4:7)

Once we see God clearly, we are able to see ourselves clearly, as God sees us. When we see God for who he is, as our creator who loved us before he formed us in the womb, we are free to look fearlessly in the mirror to recognize our God-given gifts and limitations. We see our God-ordained priorities, relationships, hopes, fears and dreams.

When we are in right relationship with God, he puts us in right relationship with others. The pieces of our lives fall into place.

Amazingly, we begin to see God's face in our own, and we see a familiar friend. "We, who with unveiled faces all reflect God's glory, are being transformed into his likeness with ever-increasing glory." (2 Cor. 3:18)

This is an awesome responsibility and privilege, knowing that we can reflect God's image to others.

Once we discover God in prayer, we see him in creation, especially in other people. "God created man in his image, in the image of God he created him, male and female he created them." (Genesis 1:27)

God's face is obvious in saints like Mother Theresa. He is equally visible in a newborn child, a suckling mother, a hardworking father, a praying nun, a devout brother, or a humble priest.

Looking closer, we see the face of God disguised in people we overlooked: the childless, the fatherless, and the grieving.

God is also apparent in the depressed, discouraged, and downhearted. He lives in the beggar, the diseased, the ugly, the handicapped, and the unborn.

With new eyes, we cast our gaze on the outcasts of society: the thief, the liar, the adulterer, the murderer, and the imprisoned. God's face is almost entirely masked in these people.

Finally, we look upon our enemies, those who hurt us. Can we see the face of God in them, however obscure?

This is the ultimate test of love, to look upon our enemies with the love of God. "Love your enemies," Jesus said, "and pray for those who persecute you." (Matthew 5:44)

I pray that I find the face of God in everyone. Let me be transformed, Lord, so that I become a reflection of your radiant face to the world.

Let people see a glimpse of God in my face. It may be the only glimpse of God they get this entire week.

O Lord, let me see your divine face in everyone I meet, and let me be a reflection of your face to a joyful and sorrowful world.

†

A loving face
in the mirror

Is that a crack in my mirror?

No, the flaw is mine; a wrinkle in my face. The closer I look, the more I see. Lamenting my imperfections, I turn away in dismay.

I wonder what Jesus' face looked like. Did he have wrinkles? What color were his eyes?

While Jesus was perfectly divine, he was humanly vulnerable, wounded by whip and thorn, scarred by nail and sword.

What would it have been like to sit near Jesus and see his face clearly?

Perhaps he was handsome, but maybe not. Maybe he looked ordinary, with a sunburned face and rough-hewn hands from his carpentry work.

Surely, his eyes sparkled with wisdom and love like two pools of sunlit water.

No doubt, Jesus' smile radiated good cheer and invited people to come near.

As I see him in my mind's eye, I recall his astounding words; "Whoever has seen me has seen the father... I am in the Father, and the Father is in me" (John 14:9).

How wonderful to think that anyone who gazed upon the face of Jesus also saw God at the same time!

I wish I had been there to see him.

Oh well, I guess I will have to wait until I get to heaven to get a really good look at Jesus. "Now we see but a poor reflection as in a mirror; then we shall see face to face" (1 Corinthians 13:12).

On the other hand, perhaps we can see him clearly right now.

Jesus promised to show himself to anyone who loves him; "Whoever loves me will be loved by my Father, and I too will love him and reveal myself to him" (John 14:21).

Therefore, if we love Jesus with a pure heart, we may expect to see his face clearly.

But wait, there is more; "If anyone acknowledges that Jesus is the Son of God, God lives in him and he in God. God is love. Whoever lives in love lives in God, and God in him" (1 John 4:15).

What a wonderful promise and a marvelous vision to contemplate – God may dwell in us, and we may dwell in God.

But how can we know this for sure?

"This is how we know that he lives in us: we know it by the Spirit he gave us" (1 John 3:23).

Now we perceive this great mystery more clearly; we may be indwelled by all three persons of the Trinity: the Father, the Son and Holy Spirit.

So the next time you see someone doing something kind or loving for Christ's sake, you may look at that person and think, "Here I see a reflection of the face of Jesus" or "This person reveals God's love."

In the same way, when you are inspired to act in a Christ-like way to others, you may think, "I am representing the Father, Son and Holy Spirit."

Even if you are blind or infirm, paralyzed or imprisoned, others may still observe in you the holy likeness of God.

After all, our blessed Creator intended our likeness as a visible sign of his extraordinary love; "In his image he created them, male and female he created them." (Genesis 1:22).

No wonder we are simultaneously thrilled and confused, humbled and exalted, transparent and transcendent.

"We, who with unveiled faces all reflect the Lord's glory, are being transformed into his likeness with ever-increasing glory, which comes from the Lord, who is the Spirit" (2 Corinthians 3:18).

So the next time you look in the mirror, look more carefully. You may be pleasantly surprised to see yourself as Jesus sees you. You may also catch a fleeting glimpse of the loving face of God.

Listen carefully
to hear God's voice

An old man was talking to his neighbor, telling him about the new hearing aid he just got.

"It cost a fortune, but it was worth it. It works perfectly."

"Really," said the neighbor. "What kind is it?"

The old man replied, "Ten thirty."

Like the man in this joke, we sometimes need to hear more clearly.

When we are lonely, worried or confused, we wish we could hear God better. We yearn to hear His voice of comfort, encouragement and guidance.

God wants you to hear His voice. Do you know that? Listen now.

To hear God clearly, first we need to be quiet. Just as Jesus left behind the noisy crowds to hear His Father's voice in the desert, we must abandon our feverish quest for news, noise and entertainment. We need to turn off our computers, televisions and cell phones, and enter into the quiet majesty of the cathedral of our souls.

As we grow accustomed to the silence, our ears become more sensitive. We may contemplate the fact that, in the beginning, God actually spoke the universe into existence; "Let there be light, and there was light" (Genesis 1:3). Therefore, we may hear God's words in all creation, whispering to us in a gentle breeze or the surging seas.

Next, we recall that God spoke each of us into being, so in some mysterious way, we embody His life-giving voice. Thus, we may hear God speaking within us, in a deeply heartfelt and mystical way. Alternatively, we may hear God speaking to us through others, if they speak in love. Therefore, God may talk to us faintly through prophets, angels, spouses, children, family members, friends, even strangers.

How is God speaking to you today? What do you hear?

17

God may speak directly to you, just like he did to Adam and Eve in the Garden; what a treat for ears to hear!

God spoke to prophets like Moses (to tell him the Ten Commandments) and to ordinary people in the Old Testament. When God spoke to Elijah, he spoke with a "still small voice" (1 Kings 19:12). God speaks to us today, in the same way. Can you hear him?

God spoke most clearly to us through His son Jesus, whom he sent to tell us the good news about the forgiveness of sins and eternal life in heaven. To hear these comforting words of Jesus, we simply open the New Testament, and his message of love engulfs us!

Jesus actually delivered an even more astonishing message when he told us that he is the Word of God made flesh. We may receive this Living Word of God in the Eucharist in a way that is infinitely intimate and overwhelms our senses.

Jesus also authorized and empowered His disciples to speak to us in His Name, so we may hear Jesus' words spoken to us by priests when we receive the Sacraments.

Finally, Jesus sent the Holy Spirit to dwell in each of us, so we may hear God speaking to us daily in the secret places and most cherished depths our souls.

We know God passionately desires us; "If anyone hears my voice and opens the door, I will come in" (Revelation 3:20).

When at last we can sit in quiet prayer and hear the voice of God everywhere, we realize that our lives are filled with a magnificent symphony of God's loving words in endless prayer.

As we listen, we recognize God's life-giving voice, always surrounding us and astounding us, with enchanting echoes of Eden and joyful revelations of the Kingdom of Heaven.

"He who has ears, let him hear" (Matthew 11:15).

Seek and you will find God

One of my earliest memories is hunting for Easter eggs at age four with my family.

I vividly recall the sunny scene that day; I was dressed in my best Sunday church clothes, and I eagerly ran through the soft green grass.

I remember exclaiming, "A red one! A blue one! A yellow one!"

As I discovered each new egg, carefully hidden, a new world revealed itself to me.

The wonderful colors and smoothness of each egg saturated my senses. I grasped each newfound treasure as a priceless gift of pure gold.

My siblings searched nearby, shouting with excitement. My parents gave us little clues, and family dogs romped underfoot.

I enjoyed a feeling of indescribable delight as I placed each egg in my basket. My joy knew no bounds, and I was filled with the newness of life.

If you are searching for a deeper faith, or if God seems to be hiding from you, it may help to think of faith like an Easter egg.

Faith is a multi-colored gem, perfectly formed, a priceless pearl of great value, "like a treasure buried in a field" (Matthew 13:44).

It is freely given by a loving parent, and gladly received by a grateful child.

Faith is carefully hidden just out of sight by our heavenly Father, but meant to be found by each one of us.

We cannot find faith unless we seek it like a child. As Jesus said, "I give praise to you, Father, Lord of heaven and earth, for although you have hidden these things from the wise and the learned, you have revealed them to the childlike" (Matthew 11:25). Therefore, we must seek our faith with exhilaration and youthful abandon.

Because it is hidden, we must actively seek our faith.

Usually faith is easy to find, and we find it the moment we seek it. This is because our Lord wants us to find him; "Those who seek me find me" (Proverbs 8:17). We must listen to his words and look for his clues if we want to find him.

Yet sometimes faith is hard to find. Sometimes a tree must be climbed. Sometimes it just takes time. Once I discovered an egg in my father's coat pocket, and that was especially fine.

Faith can be concealed in places we do not expect. If we are not looking for it, we may not see it. If we rush, we overlook a red egg among red tulips, or a yellow egg nesting under daffodils.

Prior to finding our faith, we live dimly, like spiritual embryos, in misty and concealed places.

When we discover our faith, it awakens us from our deep sleep, and fills us with delight. Then we rejoice to behold the marvelous gift of God's universe. This brings God great joy, since it is his gift to each one of us personally.

Once found, we share our faith with others. We do not hoard it in a basket for our delight alone. If one of our siblings in Christ is having trouble finding faith, we freely offer him our abundance.

Like an egg, our faith is both the symbol and reality of our new life. It is our inspiration, and our essential food for life.

In faith, we find our perfect form, and in God, we find our souls reborn.

A never-ending gift of God, our faith gives us new life forever; "Whoever believes in the Son has eternal life" (John 3:36).

As you search for faith in God, remember the wonderful joy of hunting for Easter eggs when you were young, and remember what Jesus promised; "Seek and you will find." (Matthew 7:7)

Find joy in life
and blessings today

I met a friend for lunch and our favorite waiter, a humble man named Moses, served us.

As Moses wrote down our order, he smiled.

My friend asked; "Moses, why are you always smiling?"

Without hesitating, Moses replied, "Because it's easier!"

He disappeared with our order while I laughed, and my friend laughed too.

Three people at the next table overheard us, and they smiled.

"That man," I declared, "has discovered the secret of life."

We all nodded in agreement, and our lunch tasted better than usual.

This modern-day Moses is indeed a wise man. His smile, like a pebble tossed into a lake, ripples outward to make life better, touching people he does not even know.

Joy is like that.

Some say the fluttering wings of a butterfly can start a chain reaction that results in a life-giving rainstorm on the other side of the planet. I believe this.

Yesterday I visited my parents and found them working in their garden. They labored with delight, as our original parents must have done when they tended their garden in Eden.

My mother, true to her nature, spontaneously broke into a well-known Broadway song and dance; "You've got to accentuate the positive, eliminate the negative, and latch on to the affirmative, don't mess with Mr. In-Between."

My father quickly joined her in this recreation, and they finished with a kiss among the flowers and bumblebees.

Is it any wonder that I consider it a privilege to be their son?

Of all the people I meet, the people I most enjoy are glad to be alive.

Abraham Lincoln said, "People are about as happy as they make up their minds to be."

Perhaps the most joy-filled people I have ever known are the nuns living at the Carmelite Monastery on Clayton Road in St. Louis.

Like the nuns in the movie "The Sound of Music," they live a consecrated life, separated from the world. They have gladly sacrificed everything that we crave and grasp so desperately; sex, money, power, and prestige.

Nevertheless, beyond all worldly explanation, they are joyful, each and every one, giving themselves wholeheartedly to our Lord with thanksgiving.

If you visit their chapel and listen carefully, you will hear them singing softly in the background, songs of gladness and praise.

They pray for you and me, and for the whole world, so they touch all of us deeply, in a hidden way, whether we know it or not.

They create an oasis of joy that radiates outward.

Like my parents, they help me believe that the surest sign of a Christian is joy.

What is the source of joy? Believing that we are children of God, infinitely forgiven and eternally beloved, created for a wonderful purpose beyond our understanding, destined to share in God's joys and sorrows, for the sake of the world, and for the salvation of souls.

When I think of Jesus, I think of him smiling at the whole world, spreading this good news.

Even when we frown at him, Jesus opens his heart and offers us forgiveness and infinite joy. When we spit on him, he points us lovingly to the way, the truth, and the life.

James counsels us to "Consider it all joy, my brethren, when you encounter various trials." (James 1:2)

Paul calls joy one of the fruits of the Spirit, and pleads with us to "Speak to one another with psalms, hymns, and spiritual songs... sing and make music in your heart to the Lord." (Ephesians 5:19)

So put a smile on your face knowing that you are loved by God, and "enter into the joy of your Lord" (Matthew 25:21).

†

I saw God
in church today

I caught a glimpse of God in church today.

I was sitting in a pew at an ordinary Mass, lost in thought and prayer.

I was vaguely aware of the priest saying the familiar words "This is my body" and "This is the cup of my blood."

When everyone in my row stood up for Communion, I joined them.

As I approached the priest giving out the Hosts, I noticed an older woman standing to his side offering the chalice for all to drink.

Her face was extraordinarily radiant and her eyes glistened with tears. She seemed filled with all the sorrow and joy in the world, nearly overflowing with the sanctity and holiness of the moment.

She appeared ready to laugh and cry at the same time, like someone who has just received impossibly good news, beyond expectation, and wishes to shout it from the rooftops.

She appeared mindful of the great privilege and responsibility of holding the living Christ before her, while most of us seemed to take this miracle for granted.

As she held up the Cup of Life for each person to drink, she glowed with the eternal youth of inner beauty, luminous from within. She was full of grace; the Lord was with her.

She seemed extra-aware of what she was doing; offering the natural wine transformed into the real presence of Jesus, the life-giving Blood of Christ. We often take this for granted, don't we?

I thought of the words spoken by Jesus 2,000 years ago; "This is the cup of my blood, the blood of the new and everlasting covenant, which will be shed for you and for all, so that sins may be forgiven."

This ordinary woman actually looked angelic, freshly kissed by the Son and transported into our midst. Others began to notice and stare.

Her face shone with a beatific smile, as if she had seen the face of God and now reflected it. In her face, I glimpsed the veiled beauty of the feminine image of God.

As I approached her, I noticed a painting on the wall above that portrayed our Holy Mother holding her baby Jesus.

The living woman standing before me clearly represented a present-day Madonna, a blood relative to our familiar Mother in the painting.

Her countenance looked like the Blessed Virgin as she offered me the cup containing the healing blood of Christ.

I took the cup and drank from it, aware of her gentle gaze upon me.

For a moment, I experienced the loving presence of God, and felt my heart revived with gratitude.

Once back in my pew, I watched in amazement as she served others and affected them in a similar way.

Some were visibly bewildered and looked misty-eyed as they returned to their pews. One blushed with surprise, like a child who has just been voted most popular in school.

Still others appeared dazzled, as if they had come face to face with the Divine.

As everyone sat in silence after Communion that day the quiet seemed more serene, our prayers more profound, the Spirit more present.

Afterward in the parking lot smiles appeared more genuine, greetings more heartfelt, and families more united.

I will never forget that woman's face. Whenever I think of her, she brings peace to my spirit and joy to my soul.

She reminds me that God is more intimately present to us in our daily lives than we realize. Surely, we are living miraculous lives, sharing an eternal destiny that far exceeds our expectations.

PRAYING

*"If you ask the Father
for anything in My name,
he will give it to you."*

- Jesus

Just call his name, God is here

A friend told me a true story about a 2-year old girl who wakes up every morning and softly whispers "Daddy, here."

Sure enough, her father appears at her bedside to deliver hugs and kisses.

She is too young to understand the electronic intercom on the side of her crib which allows her father to hear every sound she makes.

She only knows that when she calls, day or night, he appears.

This little girl knows she is loved. Blessed with a father who responds to her, she knows beyond the shadow of a doubt that she is a cherished and adored member of the family.

Because she has experienced the love of her earthly father, she will find it easier to trust in the ultimate goodness and loving presence of her heavenly father. Trust in one person engenders trust in another. This trust in her Lord will comfort, guide and bless her, as long as she abides in him.

When she calls "Daddy, here" she is saying a very short version of the prayer Jesus gave us; "Our father, who art in heaven, hallowed be thy name, thy kingdom come…"

In this prayer, Jesus invites us to call God by his most intimate name "Abba" which could be translated as "Daddy."

The Creator of the Universe wants us to call him "Daddy."

What does this reveal about his personality and the kind of relationship he seeks with us?

He wants us to trust him, stay close to him and love him as he loves us. He is not a far distant tyrant or dictator. He is near and dear, ready to appear and banish all fear.

This innocent little girl calls her earthly father with the same heartfelt name she will soon call God, reminding us that "God sent the spirit of his Son into our hearts, crying out, 'Abba, Father!'" (Galations 4:6)

Later in life, if she decides to stray from God's love, as we all tend to do by seeking our own will apart from his, she may suffer hurt and desolation.

However, she will find it easier than most to recall his name. She may remember that Jesus cried out to God when he was on the cross.

Then she will call upon his holy name to forgive her trespasses and to help her forgive those who trespass against her.

To her relief, God will appear in never-ending ways, fulfilling his promise that "everyone who calls on the name of the Lord will be saved" (Romans 10:13).

Happily reunited with her Lord once more, she will rest her soul by his side, knowing that he will lead her not into temptation, but will deliver her from evil.

As she grows into womanhood, she may ask God to be her knight with steed, her guide with daily feed.

Guardian of her virtue and protector of her dignity, the Lord will be her haven of rest and promoter of her best.

All the days of her life, she will marvel at his power as redeemer, provider, best friend, and uniter.

Such is the power of his Divine love, that once it is known it becomes quite unforgettable, always accessible, and finally, irresistible.

Every day he beckons us, invites us and enchants us into his familiar embrace.

Once you experience the love of God you discover power in weakness, forgiveness in sin and transformation in pain.

One of the greatest adventures in life is to discover this authentic trust in God.

So the next time you find yourself anxious, lonesome or full of fear, just close your eyes for a moment and say "Daddy, here."

Then wait in joyful hope for your heavenly Father to appear.

†

The best sermon
I never heard

As soon as the old priest started his sermon, I knew it was going to be boring.

He began speaking with a faltering voice and proceeded to tell an obscure story that made no sense to me at all. I was quickly lost and distracted.

This was not my usual church. I was travelling and had just dropped in for evening Mass.

However, I knew right away that this sermon was going to be one of the worst ever. The priest seemed unprepared, vague, and detached.

So I tuned him out, and started fuming inside my head. Slowly I became more incensed than the incense burning near the altar.

"Why didn't he prepare better?" I fumed to myself. "Don't they train these guys in Seminary? Here we are, after 2,000 years of Church history, and our priests still have not figured out how to give a decent homily! No wonder our faith is so weak; it's because the sermons are so bad!"

I seethed like a cartoon character who suffers under a dark cloud raining daggers and lightning bolts.
I sat there in silent protest, stupefied and resentful, gnashing my teeth. If I had been sitting in the back pew, I would have been tempted to sneak out.

After what seemed like an eternity, the priest finally ended his sermon. I do not remember a single word he said. It was that boring. Unfortunately, for the rest of the Mass my mind wandered aimlessly along dark paths of indignation and disgust.

After Mass ended, I walked to my car in the parking lot. No longer able to contain my protest, I complained aloud to a man walking beside me; "What did you think of that sermon?"

He walked in silence beside me, lost in thought. Then he gave a gentle reply; "That was the most beautiful sermon I ever heard."

I was stunned, and looked up at him, expecting to see him grinning sarcastically. To my astonishment, I saw that he was weeping. His face was tear-stained, and his eyes glistened in the twilight.

Suddenly embarrassed, I asked what he meant.

He thought for a moment, then responded with a smile; "I've spent most of my life estranged from God, going my own way, and doing my own thing. Last year I found him, or rather, he found me, and now I find him speaking to me in the most wonderful ways. Like that sermon we just heard. It was all about waking up, and listening, and hearing God in new ways. That describes my life, and the love I have found."

In the face of this testimony, I was speechless. I shook his hand sheepishly and thanked him. "He may not speak to me, but he speaks to thee," I thought.

As I drove home, I marveled at how God could use such a dull and ordinary priest to speak in such an extraordinary way to one of his beloved.

What is meaningless for me to hear, and a cross for me to bear, may be the fruitful words of life to a person sitting near.

Now I am a more humble and appreciative listener. Ever since that experience years ago, I cannot hear a boring sermon without imagining that someone, somewhere out there in the pews may be wiping a tear from their eye and smiling.

They may be hearing the voice of God speaking directly into their hearts, with healing words raining down on them like a spring shower on a dry and thirsty desert.

"God thunders with His voice wondrously, doing great things which we cannot comprehend." (Job 37:5)

Give and receive
the gift of listening

A country farmer had a mule with ears so long they scraped the ceiling of his small barn.

He jacked up the corners of the building and shoved flat stones under it. It was backbreaking labor that made the ramshackle barn even more unstable.

His son suggested it might be easier to dig out a few inches of the dirt floor.

"Son, it ain't the mule's legs that's too long," the farmer replied, "it's them ears."

We all know someone like this farmer, who just will not listen. It may be a spouse, parent, child, co-worker, priest, teacher, or friend.

We try every possible way to communicate with them, every appeal, and every angle. Nothing works.

Some people just refuse to open up. They will not see the light, because they do not want to see the light.

We want to help them; we try to assist them, but they choose not to listen.

Ironically, they do not realize we can help make their lives easier and increase their joy.

They do not understand, they do not "stand under", in order to see a new perspective. They lack the virtue of empathy.

Like the farmer, they think they know best, and they are not going to listen to anyone else.

This "mule-headed" attitude was expressed by Teddy Roosevelt, who said, "I don't know what other people think, I only know what they should think."

People like this can become great leaders and enjoy worldly prosperity, but their selfishness can make life unpleasant for the rest of us.

Consider Saint Paul, who single-mindedly pursued the early Christians to persecute and execute them. He thought he was doing the right thing by helping the Romans keep order in their Empire.

It took an act of God to "snap Paul out of it" on the road to Damascus. God blinded Paul with an intense light. Later the scales fell from Paul's eyes, he saw clearly for the first time, and he was born again.

The frustration we feel with obstinate people must be the same aggravation God feels toward us at times.

Am I stubborn? Has anyone told me recently that I am not listening? How can I be a better listener? Have I been on my knees today to listen to God?

The Bible is full of stories about people who refuse to listen to God. Again and again, God implores us to listen to him: "Be careful to listen to all these words which I command you, so that it may be well with you and your offspring forever." (Deut. 12:28)

Adam and Eve turned a deaf ear to God and were exiled from the Garden of Eden. The Israelites turned away from God to worship golden idols and wandered in the desert for 40 years. Jonah detoured from his mission and was swallowed by a whale. The disciples exasperated Jesus by failing to hear his message.

The good news is that once we turn to God and lend him our ears our lives get better, we gain courage and wisdom to listen to others, and our relationships blossom like flowers.

God promises to listen to us when we pray. Perhaps we can return the favor by listening to him.

O Lord, make me a better listener.

Open my eyes and my ears; give me a teachable heart.

Give me empathy and understanding, and help me ease the burden of others.

†

Dying to live
more joyfully

I have journeyed through the night to awaken early this morning in one of my favorite places on earth.

Although it is pitch dark, I arise to the sound of the clanging steeple bell at 3:30 AM. My tired body rebels, but I insist.

Though I am greeted with the lonely kiss of cold upon my cheek, and my legs are unsteady beneath me, I smile in quiet anticipation.

I stumble down the hall, dip my fingers into the holy water, and slide into a pew in the darkened chapel. I am glad to show my body who is master.

I bend my knees, fold my hands, and bow my head.

Shadowy figures gather around me in silence.

Surrounded by these strange friends, my breathing grows easier, and more natural.

Suddenly the light comes on; it hurts my closed eyes, and I command myself to stand.

The familiar chord is played, and I join my voice in gently chanting the ancient words with the others: "Oh Lord, come to my assistance, make haste to help me."

Thus I find myself at peace in the early mist surrounding the Trappist monks at Assumption Abbey, a monastery deep in the secluded hills of southern Missouri. (www.assumption abbey.org)

For me it is a welcome relief from a noisy world. A chance to decompress. To reflect. To find that extra grace needed to kick free of all those hungry habits which come between me and my Lord.

I must confess that at other times of the year I am unlikely to accept suffering gracefully; I share the Cross grudgingly.

Lent is different, a special time when I voluntarily decide to die to myself, to pick up my cross daily, and follow him.

I marvel at the fact that I can live in the imitation of Christ. In my own small way I am following in His footsteps, sharing His 40 days in the wilderness.

In Lent, I discover that "It is no longer I who live, but Christ who lives in me." (Gal. 2:20)

I find a special grace from You during this time of year, Lord. At other times, I am not quite so brave, not so holy.

I think of You in Heaven, Jesus, and the fact that You did not have to come to earth, or suffer indignity and death. You could have called all the angels to rescue You. However, You chose to condescend to earth, to live humbly with your beloved children, sharing all our joys and sorrows. Can I do less? I would like to do more. For Your sake, for my sake, for the sake of the whole world, I would like to do more - like these holy monks.

They are some of the most joyful men I have ever met, these monks who have set themselves apart from the world.

Like Robin Hood and his band of merry men. Except they steal from no one, take from no one; they only give. They spend their lives in work and in prayer, for you and for me, and for the whole world.

They harken back to an ancient time, before the Dark Ages, when the world was lit only by candles and fire, and the sacred words of our Lord were kept alive by monks, monasteries, and manuscripts.

They also herald the future, when everything will be illuminated by our Lord, made new by His Holy Presence.

They are living signs of that glorious future which is yours and mine.

I find it a privilege to share their life and bread for a moment, especially during Lent. They show me how wonderful it is to fast, and pray, and die to myself as Christ did, in order to live more joyfully.

Lent is one of my favorite times of the year, and it can be the same for you, too.

WORKING

*"Whatever you do,
do your work heartily,
as for the Lord."*

- St. Paul

Do not worry about money

If you are concerned about your financial security in these uncertain times, listen to the wisdom of a 100-year-old man who lived through the Great Depression. He assures visitors, "Don't worry about anything, you'll be all right."

Coming from a man who learned the hard way how to stretch a dime, his words sure are comforting.

How much more comforting to receive the same message from the God of all Creation; "Do not worry about your life, what you will eat or drink; or about your body, what you will wear" (Matthew 6:24).

You may say, "That's fine, but these are only words. How can a Bible verse pay my bills?" Consider the following true stories:

I know a man who was down on his luck and his car died. He could not afford to buy another, and he needed a car to get to work or he would lose his job.

That night he got a phone call from a high school friend who said, "I just bought a new car and I was wondering if you'd like to have my old one. It's nothing to look at, but it runs."

God knows what we need. Does he not "provide for the sparrows in the air and the lilies of the field"?

Of course, we must do our part in prayer and deed; "Go to the ant, study her ways and learn wisdom" (Proverbs 6:6).

We must listen more carefully for God's quiet voice and let our hardships draw us nearer to him and each other.

Then we will hear surprising words that will teach and enrich us beyond measure; "I know the plans I have for you," declares the Lord, "plans to prosper you and not to harm you, plans to give you hope and a future" (Jeremiah 29:11).

We can help by cooperating with God, by working alongside others, and praising his holy name.

When the ancient Israelites wandered in the desert, God provided them with manna from heaven, but only enough to survive for each day.

Like them we may suffer, but God cannot fill us until we are empty. Thus we learn to face our future with faith, hope and gratitude.

A single mother living on a farm with four children found herself bankrupt and facing foreclosure.

However, a businessman appeared at her door and said; "I want to buy the mineral rights on your property for $20,000. If we find oil, we will pay you a percentage of the profits. She agreed and sure enough, they found a gusher.

Are all these stories really so far-fetched, so hard to believe? Don't we hear daily about someone finding a new job, inheriting a fortune, inventing something new or writing a best-seller?

Isn't it commonplace to read about someone winning a scholarship, getting a pay raise, receiving a research grant or landing an acting job?

We have to start seeing our God as he really is; a great big God who created the universe and holds us in his hands.

We also have to see ourselves more clearly, as he sees us. We are his beloved sons and daughters, and he wants to give us the kingdom of heaven.

Imagine your father is Microsoft's Bill Gates, the richest man in the world. Suppose he said to you not to worry about your financial situation. You'd believe him, wouldn't you?

We hear the same thing from our father, the Great Provider; "I will surely make you prosper" (Genesis 32:12).

Now do you see? Do you believe? It is not magic or luck; it is the mighty hand of God, outstretched to you in love. Take hold of his hand and accept your inheritance.

'Seek ye first the kingdom of God, and his righteousness, and all these things will be given to you as well" (Matthew 6:33).

†

Finding wealth
in surprising places

One day a father from a rich family took his son on a trip to the country to glimpse how poor people live.

They spent all day at the small farm of an impoverished family.

As they drove home that night the father asked his son, "Now do you see how poor people live?"

After a pause, his son responded, "We have one dog; they have four. We have a swimming pool; they have a creek that goes on forever. We play on the driveway; they have big fields. We have streetlights; but they have the stars."

His father was quiet.

His son added, "I thought we were rich, Dad, but in some ways they are richer."

This story reminds us that we may find wealth in unexpected places. We may be rich in surprising ways.

Throughout history people have sought wealth and success. Ever since God gave Adam and Eve the responsibility to be fruitful and to subdue the earth, we know that hard work is noble. An abundant harvest is good; it allows us to provide for ourselves as well as to give to those less fortunate.

Problems arise, however, because our desire for wealth has a tendency to spin out of control. We can become obsessed with prosperity, idolizing it more than anything.

Money itself is not the problem. As St. Paul says; "the love of money is the root of all evils" (I Timothy 6:10).

Sometimes we love money more than we love God. In this we break the first commandment; "I am the Lord your God… you shall have no other gods before me." (Exodus 20:2).

Just as the ancient Israelites created a golden calf to worship instead of God, we often become consumed with a desire to acquire the finest jewelry, cars and houses. But when we seek God first, we find freedom, and contentment replaces our craving and coveting.

An inordinate craving for wealth can make us exploit other people, including the people closest to us.

Lust for money can dictate whom we marry, where we live and who we choose for friends. Even priests and nuns and monks, many of whom take vows of poverty, are tempted by wealth-related desires for power, position and privilege.

When we love wealth we are never satisfied; rather we are slaves to our desire.

To guard against becoming too attached to our possessions, we may recall that we are only temporary stewards. Then we will not slavishly store up treasures on earth, where moth and rust destroy. Our lives, Jesus warned, may end tonight.

God says he will cast down the rich and send them away empty-handed, while the poor shall be filled up.

If we become conceited by our riches, acting as if we earned it or somehow deserve them, we must remember that all wealth comes from God, the source of all life. He is the One who gives us the intelligence and energy which enables us towards any material success.

By the same token, we need not be discouraged or ashamed if we are poor. Jesus counsels us to look for the ways in which we are rich in spite of our physical poverty.

We can be free of jealousy toward others and free from anxiety about what we will eat, drink or wear. God knows exactly what we need, and he will satisfy our needs in surprising ways if only we put him first.

Just as he bestows his abundance on the birds in the sky and the lilies of the field, God will provide for us.

As we decide on our priorities in life, let us focus on Jesus' wonderful promise: "Seek first the kingdom of God, and all these things will be given you besides." (Matthew 6:33).

Life is like
a roller coaster

If you find yourself worrying about the future and fearful of life's unpredictable ups and downs, remember the joyful thrill of riding on a roller coaster.

Standing in line for the world's scariest roller coaster, my friends and I pass an ominous sign that cautions; "Be afraid."

We laugh and press forward, past another menacing sign; "Be very afraid."

A third sign with a skull and crossbones contains a final warning; "I'd turn back if I were you."

This adventure is clearly not for the faint-hearted.

Our destination is a ride called "The Screaming Monster".

With growing excitement, we all jump on board, shivering with anticipation for the wild ride ahead.

Lurching forward, we ride clackety-clack up to a dizzying height.

The bravest among us shout, "Nice knowing you!" and show off by raising their hands to the sky, defying gravity, tempting fate, and proclaiming; "I am not afraid!"

The mere mortals among us ride with our eyes squeezed tight, holding on for dear life, and our knuckles turning white.

Suddenly we jolt, and slide into a terrifying, heart-racing, 200-foot drop, followed by two upside-down loop-de-loops, with alternating darkness and light.

We relish the moment as our world turns upside down, twisting and turning, and scream with a mix of terror and delight; the brave and timid alike.

We take courage in the midst of it all, knowing we are safe.

All is well, we hope, all is well.

At last we clank safely back to the platform, where we disembark with wobbly knees and windblown hair.

We greet the solid ground gratefully, and one friend kisses that ground on his hands and knees.

We are revitalized, renewed and richly blessed. With deeper friendships from our experience, we share a greater trust in the goodness of life, more courage to face the next ride, and a resounding chorus of "Let's do it again!"

Sad to say, along the roller coaster of life, some of us lose our way. We "grow up" and lose our trust in life. We forget our youthful love, our love of God.

A seven-year-old daughter was thrilled when her family took her to Disney World for the first time.

She headed straight for Space Mountain. Her father worried that the roller coaster would be too scary for her, but to his delight, she rode it twice.

The next year when the family returned to Disney World, the daughter, now eight, again dragged her parents to Space Mountain.

As they stood in line, her father could see her soberly studying the signs that warned about the ride's speed.

"Dad," she said, "I don't think I want to go."

"Why?" her father asked. "You enjoyed this ride last time."

"I know," the daughter replied, "But this year I can read better!"

Like this little girl, we start to believe the signs that say, "Be afraid." Slowly we fear for our safety. We begin to doubt that the nuts and bolts have been properly checked.

We no longer see the smiles of others, we see only terror. We become deaf to the laughter of our friends and hear only their screams of fright.

We need to relax and rediscover our youthful trust in our heavenly father, who is the original "Roller Coaster Tycoon." If we do, we can enjoy the topsy-turvy ride through the peaks and valleys of our lives trusting that our Lord is keeping us safe.

"I will lead the blind by a way they do not know; in paths they do not know I will guide them." (Isaiah 42:16)

We can trust that the nuts and bolts are safe and the seatbelts secure. Our Father is watching out for our safety.

So hold on tight to your faith in God, grab a seat, and enjoy the ride of your life.

†

Road trip with God at my side

I recently bought a car and discovered that God comes along as an option.

The owner's manual calls it a GPS "Global Positioning System," but it functions so much like God that I like to call it my "God Positioning System".

It sits high in the center of the dashboard, always in front, guiding the way. The bright screen displays a map, oriented as if you were up in the sky with an unlimited view. On this map, it pinpoints your position with a gold star. When you move, the map moves with you, and so does the gold star.

How does it work? Three satellites high in the sky automatically triangulate your position, pinpointing your exact location at all times. So the GPS always knows where you are, where you have been, where you are going, AND the best way to get you there.

Sounds a lot like God, doesn't it?

As you drive to your destination, the GPS highlights the correct roads. An arrow appears on the screen before every turn, and a voice says, "In one mile, turn right." The voice speaks any language and works in every corner of the planet.

Here is my favorite feature: if you make a wrong turn, the voice calmly says; "Please make a U-turn."

If you continue going the wrong way the voice repeats the words - "Please make a U-turn."

If you persist in your mistake, the GPS calculates your new position, highlights a new route and says, "At the next intersection, turn right." In fact, every time you miss your turn, the GPS faithfully recreates a new path, reminding you to turn at the next intersection until you safely reach your destination.

If you want to go your own way and you get lost, you must deliberately ignore and defy your GPS. Follow it, and you never miss the mark. I do not know how I ever found my way without it…

Isn't that just like God?

If you feel lost, or find that you need help deciding the right direction in your life, remember that God wants to help you find your way; "Your father in heaven is not willing that any of these little ones should be lost" (Matthew 18:14).

In what way is God asking you to follow him today? Will you trust him, even in unfamiliar territory, perhaps without a map?

Consider how the ancient people of the Bible trusted God for direction. Moses led the Israelites out of captivity, and "the Lord preceded them, in the daytime by means of a column of cloud to show them the way, and at night by means of a column of fire" (Exodus 13:21). Noah in his Ark trusted a dove to find land. The Three Wise Men followed a bright star in the night sky to find the baby Jesus.

Years later, Jesus gave his disciples the Holy Spirit as a guide to help them change the world's direction.

We receive the Holy Spirit during the sacrament of Confirmation. This wonderful Spirit inside us is Love, for God is Love. Thus each of us is guided by this Love, if we allow God and his love to direct us.

That is good news for me, because I often make wrong turns in my life. It comforts me to know God is always there to help me get back on the right track. I gladly choose the option to have the Creator of the universe next to me, guiding me every step of the way.

"You guide me along the right path for the sake of your name. Even when I walk through a dark valley, I fear no harm for you are at my side" (Psalm 23).

FORGIVING

"Forgive them, Father,
for they know not what they do."

- Jesus

How to handle
the hurts in life

A young boy wrote this letter to God: "Dear God, did you really mean, 'Do unto Others as They Do unto You?' Because if you did, then I am going to get even with my brother. Signed, Daniel."

We all know the pain of being hurt by someone. Whether by enemies, friends or loved ones, all trespasses hurt.

Years ago, I suffered an offense that was especially grievous. It felt like a flaming arrow shot into my back, beyond my reach to pull it out.

I tried to get over it with prayer, fasting, forgetting, exercise, distractions and entertainment. Nothing seemed to work.

I probably appeared to others like a cartoon character with black clouds, torrential rains and thunderbolts following me everywhere.

Robbed of my joy, I saw only darkness at midday.

Seeking consolation, I finally stumbled into church. Entering the confessional booth, I saw the familiar face of a benevolent old priest. He welcomed me, then closed his eyes and folded his hands, awaiting my confession.

I choked out broken sentences explaining my predicament. I spoke of the offense that had wounded me so deeply and lamented that, in my sorrow and resentment I was experiencing a broken relationship with God, like a total eclipse of the Son.

He nodded in silence, smiled and said, "Let it remind you of your total dependence on our Lord."

I paused and waited for more enlightenment.

When it became obvious that the priest would say no more, I inquired, "That's it?"

"Yes," he replied. "Now your penance is to say the Our Father for someone who needs it the most." Then he spoke the blessing of Christ's forgiveness.

I thanked him and left.

Finding a pew in the empty chapel, I knelt on the floor, wanting earnestly to depend on God.

Unable to decide whom to pray for, because many people needed it, including me, I decided to let God decide.

I prayed "Our Father, who art in heaven…" and found myself breathing deeper, rediscovering God's truth that nothing happens to us outside the ordained or permitted will of our Creator.

God promises that he works everything together for our good.

We know that everything is within his providence, working for our good and the good of the whole world. Therefore we rejoice even in darkness, pain and suffering.

Jesus shows us the way; "Love your enemies, do good to those who hate you, bless those who curse you, pray for those who mistreat you." (Luke 6:28)

We say these words, but can we truly live them? Yes. Even as he endured the pain of betrayal, desertion, and crucifixion, Jesus cried, "Lord, forgive them, for they know not what they do."

In contrast to Jesus, I had been reacting to the offense with a prideful heart, a hard heart that God wished to break so that he could replace it with a heart of flesh. Slowly and reluctantly, I became more aware of my hidden pride and my own trespasses.

Now my penance offered new healing; "Forgive us our trespasses, as we forgive those who trespass against us." With divine assistance my prayer released my offender, liberated me, and restored my relationship with God.

As I prayed "Thy Kingdom come, Thy will be done…" I glimpsed an exhilarating vision of how freeing and redeeming it would be to actually live a life of perfect forgiveness by flying above the dark clouds of division.

A shaft of sunlight shone through a stained glass window and burst into colors on my folded hands. A couple of tears on the floor sparkled like dropped diamonds.

With a spring in my step, I walked out the front door into dazzling sunlight. A young boy sailed past me on his bicycle, his dog running alongside, and on a branch overhead, a dove cooed softly.

Open the door to forgiveness and joy

One of the blessings of the Sacrament of Reconciliation is the fact that it teaches us, at a very young age, how to say the magic words "I'm sorry."

Take the boy who goes to Reconciliation and tells the priest he is sorry for kicking his brother.

As a teenager, he admits to his father that he stole some money from his wallet.

As a husband, he asks his wife to forgive him for being aloof and insensitive.

As a father, he apologizes to his son for losing his temper.

As an old man, he kneels alone in the back of the church, and asks God to forgive him for his sins. He wipes a tear from his eye, forgiven and renewed once more, and gives thanks.

In this way, forgiveness redeems those who ask for and then receive it.

Many families teach their children to resolve conflicts verbally. They expect their kids to talk out problems, and they encourage reconciliation.

Ever since The Fall, unfortunately no family is perfect. Everyone fights. But at the end of the day healthy families "circle the wagons around the campfire", and reconcile over supper.

Some families do not practice forgiveness, so the children never learn how to apologize or forgive others.

For those who never learned, scripture teaches us how to forgive and find joy. First, we pray for the ability to forgive others, and God helps us.

We contemplate the fact that God sometimes allows other people to offend us, not because he wants us to suffer, but to encourage us to forgive others, as he forgives us.

We do well to consider that God can use hurtful people to redirect our gaze away from the suffering they cause us and toward him, so that we may learn forgiveness by contemplating and imitating His example.

We remember what Jesus taught: that members of our family consist also of other believers. This opens us to healing and counsel from fellow believers.

Finally, we meditate on the fact that Jesus forgave His persecutors as he hung on the cross crying, "Lord, forgive them, for they know not what they do."

We know we are forgiving someone when we unshackle from ourselves any anger and bitterness he caused us. Joy returns to our lives. We take a deep breath and release the person who offended us to God's care; thereby enjoying peace and thanksgiving.

We know we are receiving God's grace to forgive someone when we feel ourselves moving "from resentment to gratitude," as Henri Nouwen said.

Our lives then resemble the story of a family surrounding their beloved grandfather. With the help of eager grandchildren, he unwraps a long red stick.

"Just what I wanted," he exclaims, "a backscratcher!"

His little granddaughter shouts, "Let me do it!" He gives it to her, and she scratches his back. Then she says, "Somebody scratch my back, too!" Another grandson leaps to his feet.

Spontaneously, everyone jumps up to join the others. A circle forms with each one laughing and scratching the back of the person in front. Even the dogs join in with their barking and wagging of tails.

This story gives us a glimpse of heaven; the way God originally intended life on earth to be, before The Fall. We also find healing when we allow others to scratch our back, and in turn we scratch theirs. We relax, and see the world anew with loving eyes. Our cups are filled to overflowing.

We know the joy of forgiveness when we "find tongues in trees, books in the running brooks, sermons in stones, and good in everything," as Shakespeare said.

Then we rejoice with each other and say, "I will praise God's name in song and glorify him with thanksgiving." (Psalm 69:30)

50

✝

God wants you to enjoy His best

A mother was preparing pancakes for her two young sons. The boys began to argue over who would get the first pancake.

To teach them a moral lesson, their mother announced, "If Jesus was sitting here, he would say 'Let my brother have the first pancake, I can wait.'

Immediately one brother turned to his sibling and said, "Okay, I'll go first. You be Jesus!"

We can all recognize a little bit of that self-interest in ourselves, can't we?

We all want to be first in line, first to choose, first to decide what we want.

While we know Jesus is generous and promises to give us what is best for us, we still want to choose selfishly.

We are afraid Jesus will give us a smaller slice of life than we want, or a distasteful portion, so we rush ahead of others to try to choose our own way.

In our reluctance to trust God, we often disregard others and ignore our own best interests.

However, we should not condemn ourselves for distrusting God's plans. Let us remember that Jesus, in his humanity, pleaded with God to be spared crucifixion; "My Father, if it is possible, may this cup be taken from me…"

Jesus was so afraid of his destiny that he sweated drops of blood. Have you ever been this anxious?

Still, in the same breath, Jesus quickly opened himself to his Father's will, trusting his Father to give him only what was most loving, most good, and most perfect; "…yet not as I will, but as you will" (Matthew 26:39).

By imitating Jesus, we can find peace in the midst of any trial or storm.

When we are afraid or worried about the future we can find a quiet moment to ask God for exactly what we want, but then we must gracefully release everything to his perfect will.

You may say, "That's impossible! Jesus is God but I am only human. You don't know the trouble I'm in!"

You are correct; in our fallen state, we all find it difficult to trust God. In the natural, we instinctively grasp at pancakes.

We need God's help to learn to trust him.

To increase our trust in God, we have many prayers to help us. "O God, come to my assistance, make haste to help me."

Our most powerful aid in trust-building is the Eucharist. Jesus said, "Whoever eats my flesh and drinks my blood has eternal life" (John 6:54). His disciples complained that this was a hard teaching to understand, and many of them departed as a result.

Nevertheless, the disciples who stayed with Jesus discovered "the peace of God that transcends all understanding" (Phil. 4:7).

They discovered that Jesus truly had their best interests at heart.

Then Jesus sent them out into the world to spread the Good News of eternal life. In effect he said to his disciples to go out and be Jesus to the world.

So enjoy the peace and power of the Eucharist, in which we share the life of God. Pray something like this: "Jesus, I gratefully accept whatever you give me today."

Open yourself to Jesus and let him come into your life more deeply every day.

As you develop your trust in Jesus you will find yourself more joyfully giving to others, as well as allowing them to go first in line before you.

As you gain confidence that God will give you everything you need, you will discover a secret delight in allowing others to go first, seeking what is best for them, and giving them what they need.

Then in quiet prayer, you may well imagine God smiling upon you and saying, "OK, good job; you're being Jesus now!"

How to deal with
a difficult person

In one of my favorite movies "It's A Wonderful Life", a small-town banker named George Bailey suddenly faces bankruptcy and disgrace.

In desperation, he prepares to jump off a bridge into the frigid water below, but suddenly another individual leaps off in front of him. Instantly forgetting himself, George strips off his coat and dives in to save the screaming stranger.

Later, as they dry their clothes beside an old wood-burning stove, the stranger introduces himself as "Clarence Odbody, Angel Second Class."

Clarence explains that he is George's guardian angel, assigned to help George find meaning in his life. Furthermore, Clarence claims that he will earn his wings as a heavenly reward for helping George. Clarence tries his best to convince George that he currently has a wonderful life, but George is skeptical.

For the majority of the movie George distrusts, disappoints and mocks Clarence every step of the way.

Although he is continually rebuffed Clarence faithfully attends to his Assignment, repeatedly resorts to prayer, and earns his wings in the end.

Perhaps someone in your life troubles you. It may be a stranger, a trusted friend, or a family member who offended you. The offense may have been accidental or intentional, recently or a long time ago. You may feel frustrated, angry and resentful.

As difficult as it may be to believe, this person may be your Assignment. As preposterous and repugnant as it may seem, you may have been given a mission, like Clarence, to help this person in some way.

"No way!" you may say. "This person is hopeless!"

You may think you can never forget the deep wound inflicted by this person, whether it was emotional, financial, physical or spiritual.

However, if you forget yourself for a moment and look past your hurt, you may recall Jesus' words; "You have heard that it was said, 'You shall love your neighbor and hate your enemy.' But I say to you, love your enemies, and pray for those who persecute you" (Matthew 5:44).

This may seem outrageous and disgraceful. Your tormentor may be the last person on earth you would choose to help. Nevertheless, you may be the one person who can lead this troublemaker to God.

Your assignment may be as simple as being nice to the person whenever you meet him..

Then again it may require you to walk the extra mile.

You may need to practice Clarence-like virtues such as humility, patience, kindness and forgiveness. You may be surprised to discover new depths of courage, wisdom and compassion deep within your heart.

Even so, it may be impractical or impossible for you to interact with the offender. In this case, you can always rely on the power of prayer. Pray that the person turns away from darkness and toward the light. Pray for that person's happiness.

Try it now, just for a moment. You may need to pray a little… or a lot! One anxious mother named Monica prayed for her sinful son for twenty-four years. Thanks to her prayers, Augustine ultimately converted and became a Saint.

You may never have the satisfaction of witnessing the good results of your prayers here on earth. The person you pray for may never thank you.

Yet God works miracles beyond space and time. Your prayers may work effectively back to the past or ahead to the future. Trust that "God works all things together for good" (Romans 8:28).

You will enjoy peace of mind, knowing you have done your best, when you truly commit that person to God's mercy and compassion.

Then you will feel your soul take flight, as if you were given angel's wings, liberated like Clarence to soar heavenward, or free like George Bailey, to live and laugh and love again.

†

We hide in fear;
He seeks in love

One morning a 3-year old boy asked his mother for some candy.

"Not until after lunch," she replied.

Shortly she noticed both he and the candy had disappeared. She called out his name, but he did not answer. She called a second time, adding that he was in big trouble if he did not tell her where he was.

A few seconds later, a little voice from the corner behind the big easy-chair said, "I don't know. I must've gone to Grandma's house."

We laugh at this story because this little boy reminds us of ourselves. We all have a tendency to be impatient, to take what is promised before it is given; and then we hide in one way or another.

On a deeper level, this reminds us of our first parents, Adam and Eve, who were allowed to eat anything in the Garden of Eden except the fruit of one tree.

Regrettably, they ate the forbidden fruit and immediately hid from each other and from God. In his desire for their best, God came looking for them with love.

Why do we hide? Because we know, deep down, that we have done wrong. The light becomes a threat to our dark secret.

Those who seek relationships with us become our enemies, especially those who love us most. We fearfully separate ourselves from friends and loved ones who only desire to provide the forgiveness, healing and reconciliation we desperately need.

"The light came into the world, but people preferred darkness to light, because their works were evil. For everyone who does wicked things hates the light and does not come toward the light, so that his works might not be exposed. But whoever lives the truth comes to the light, so that his works may be clearly seen as done in God." (John 3:19)

We hide in many places and in many ways. We disguise ourselves with the artfulness of actors, the deception of thieves, and the camouflage of chameleons.

Some of us hide behind a glittering façade of beauty, wealth, power or possessions. Others hide behind a cloak of silence, rebellion, anger or complacency.

The big easy chair we hide behind may be alcohol, drugs, gambling or sex. We may even hide behind work, exercise, good deeds or religion. Whatever cloak or disguise we choose the result is the same; we separate ourselves from others and from God. Before long, we become strangers even to ourselves.

To come closer to God we may ask, "Am I hiding? In what ways? When do I feel most alone or least lovable? Who in my life is gently calling me into the fearsome but glowing light of day?" The wise counsel and encouragement of these gentle friends may help us.

Gradually we realize our trustworthy companions are calling us to enjoy God's blessings, and we find the comfort and courage to walk toward the light.

Like long-lost miners returning to the surface from underground tunnels, we emerge, squinting our eyes and blinking in the sunlight. We rejoice as we reunite with God and others. We exult as we enjoy the light of the Son.

So let us allow ourselves to be embraced by our Creator, who offers us the light of his perfect love; "God is light, and in him there is no darkness at all." (1 John 1:5)

RECONCILING

*"Be kind to one another,
tender-hearted, forgiving each other,
just as God in Christ also has forgiven you."*

- St. Paul

Love makes friends out of enemies

We all have enemies, seen and unseen.

We can be nice to everyone, but eventually we will encounter adversaries. If the nicest person who ever lived (Jesus) had enemies then we may also expect an antagonist or two.

How do we deal with them?

"The best way to destroy an enemy," said Abraham Lincoln, "is to make him a friend."

To learn how to make a friend of an enemy, let us listen to the greatest Teacher who ever lived.

Then as now, Jesus was born in a time in which people took cruel revenge on each other. The Mosaic Law was interpreted to mean that if someone hurt you, you should hurt him or her in return.

People said "An eye for an eye, and a tooth for a tooth."

Today we hear that same bitter desire for revenge when people say, "Don't get mad, get even."

Jesus introduced a radical new way of thinking.

One day he sat on a mountainside and said to his disciples; "You have heard it said, you shall love your neighbor and hate your enemy.' But I say to you, love your enemies..." (Matthew 5:43).

His listeners must have been astonished. "No way!" they probably exclaimed. "You don't know how much I hurt! He lied! She left me! He abused me! She stole from me! He killed my brother! I want revenge!"

The Great Peacemaker quietly continued, "...and pray for those who persecute you..."

This must have confounded the crowd even more. "Pray for our enemies? Why should we?"

Jesus went on to say, "...that you may be children of your heavenly Father." By loving our enemies and praying for them, we are children of God! What does this mean for us?

Jesus did not mean we cannot defend ourselves from schoolyard bullies, local thieves or foreign despots, for he admonishes us elsewhere to resist evil. His concern here is to cultivate a loving heart toward all.

We should imitate God, who loves everyone, because he created us in love. He makes the sun rise on the bad and the good, and causes rain to fall on the just and the unjust.

If we resent the fact that God blesses our enemies, we may recall that we are also rebellious toward God. Yet he reaches out and loves us first, so "while we were enemies, we were reconciled to God" (Romans 5:10).

Finally, we see the key to it all: "if God so loved us, we also must love others" (I John 4:11).

Now we delight in pleasing him by returning his favor; by loving him with all our hearts, and our neighbors as ourselves. We imitate him, as children do, and become more holy.

Then the Great Reconciler anoints us with a dewdrop of understanding on our furrowed brow, saying, "So be perfect, just as your heavenly Father is perfect."

However, we cannot be perfect without God's help. We are physically disabled and spiritually handicapped. If we are to love our enemies, we need to put on the mind of Christ.

Once we pray, and put ourselves in God's hands, the Holy Spirit comes silently to our assistance, making haste to help us. Now we are enabled to love as God loves, and we journey on the mystical way, in the direction of perfection.

Amazingly, we find ourselves loving others as God loved the world, loving all our neighbors as ourselves. Love is the answer. As we love our enemies, we become conscious that they are brothers and sisters of ours, created by our loving Father, and separated only by a lack of love.

O Lord, allow me to restore souls with your love. With your divine love, let me transform enemies into friends. Now I close my eyes in prayer and imagine your eternal love and grace as a fountain of living water, flowing through my body, rippling across my neighborhood, sweeping over distant lands, and engulfing the entire world in an irresistible wave of peace and harmony.

†

Making peace with people around you

A little boy wrote this letter to God in Sunday school, "Dear God, I bet it is very hard for you to love everybody in the whole world. There are only four people in our family and I can never seem to do it."

This boy is experiencing one of the difficult challenges in life: how to get along with other people, especially those near to you.

All families have difficulties communicating and getting along. This is the result of living in a fallen world, one in which we each tend to want our own way.

Growing up in my family, we were blessed because my parents taught us how to communicate openly and resolve conflicts.

We were not perfect, of course, but we were taught to settle our differences. Disunity and estrangement were not an option. We were expected to make peace.

So instead of brooding over whether or not to reconcile, we tried hard to practice forgiveness and conflict resolution.

For example, we were not allowed to give a careless apology. Our mother said, "Now look the other person in the eyes and mean it when you say it."

Sadly, many people get stuck at a distance from each other and never reconcile. Not only does the devil gleefully instigate this disunity, but he also perpetuates it.

Once we realize who is fanning the flames of our disunity, we find it easier to come together and to triumph over our differences.

I once met a man who attended Mass every day, but admitted "I had a fight with my brother and haven't spoken to him in forty years."

How sad, I thought, that he had not allowed the love of Jesus to heal his heart.

Jesus says, "If anyone says 'I love God' but hates his brother, he is a liar; for whoever does not love a brother whom he has seen cannot love God whom he has not seen" (I John 4:20).

We are created for love, meant for unity, and called to peace.

Remember Jesus said that the greatest commandment after loving God is "You shall love your neighbor as yourself" (Mattthew 22:36). The world is a marvelously different place when we take this to heart.

We get a beautiful reminder to practice this unity at every Mass when the priest says, "Let us offer each other the Sign of Peace."

This is a wonderful opportunity to experience the love of God. He created us to share this divine love.

I know a woman who turns around in her pew, smiling and waving to everyone in all directions. She radiates the way things were in the Garden of Eden. She is enabling God's Kingdom to come nearer to us, and also helping his will to be done.

Unfortunately, it is not always possible to make peace with everyone. Some people do not want to be reconciled, and you cannot force them. Love does not force people against their will.

Some people frown during the Sign of Peace or look down at the floor. Some are loners who seem to pray, "Give me this day my daily bread" rather than "Give us this day our daily bread."

Let us pray that Jesus will enter the hearts of these strangers as he entered the locked room where his disciples were hiding in fear. They need to hear his healing words, "Peace be with you."

As we joyfully offer the Sign of Peace to be reconciled with the family of God, may our smiles fill us with the peace and love of Christ.

This is a foretaste of our eternal life to come, a welcome glimpse of heaven on earth.

Life is like
a Merry-Go-Round

When I was five years old, the school recess bell rang every day at ten o'clock and we all ran outside to the playground.

I liked the Merry-Go-Round.

It was rickety and round, made out of wood, like a giant wagon wheel, with "spokes" radiating out from the center.

As it spun faster and faster, everyone held on to the outer rim. We all started hollering with a mixture of excitement and terror.

The world became a whirling, dizzying confusion of motion and color. Everyone's faces were lost in a blur, and their voices merged in ear-splitting screams.

Sometimes we went so fast that many kids lost their grip and flew off entirely, sprawling in the dirt. The hard stones caused tears and bloody knees. Once a classmate pried my fingers off the rail and I went tumbling off into the dirt.

One day I discovered something amazing.

As I pulled myself towards the center of the merry-go-round, the spinning began to slow. Pulling myself even closer to the center, I was able to stand up straight, and regain my balance.

Getting there was difficult, but at the very center, I felt almost motionless, as if the world stood still. I stood perfectly balanced, without even holding on, my arms outstretched. I could see and hear everything and everyone else perfectly.

With the playground spinning around me, it seemed like the center of the universe.

The center was my favorite place on the ride.

Life is a lot like a Merry-Go-Round, and God is at the center.

We hang on for dear life, as events become a dizzying blur. People crash into us, and we crash into them. Faster and faster it goes, and sometimes we cannot even recognize those closest to us. People scream and yell, and clutch on to us.

We lose our grip voluntarily or due to someone forcing us, and we go flying off into confusion. Sometimes our lives feel out of control, and in our pain we wonder, "Where is God? Does he even know or care about my suffering?"

Then we recall Jesus' comforting promise; "I am with you always." (Matthew 28:20)

We remember that God is at the center. He is in control. He created the Universe, and he has a divine plan for each of us.

As we move toward him, we journey to the center, where everything slows down. We begin to relax, we regain our balance, we can breathe deeply now, everything is all right.

Amazingly, as we move towards God at the center, we also get closer to each other. Everyone who moves toward the center also draws nearer to each other. Have you noticed that God-centered people are usually a joy to be around and easy to get along with? That is because they share the understanding of the unifying love of our Lord.

The opposite is also true; as we run away from God, along each of the "spokes" radiating outward, we also distance ourselves from each other, until we spin off into solitary oblivion and land in the dirt.

God invites us to move toward him, to find His perfect peace at the center of our lives.

There we discover our Creator and our true selves. We discover truth, tranquility, and stability. The frenzied pace of life begins to subside. We still are traveling just as far in the world, and just as fast, but without all the noise and confusion.

Then we delight in moving closer to God by obeying his will, in enjoying the Eucharist and other Sacraments, by practicing "centering" prayer, and in helping others find him.

Life is good when we move towards God at the center.

†

How to enjoy
His loving kiss

One day a grandmother gave her 4-year-old grandson a big kiss on his cheek.

When he brushed his hand against the damp spot she smiled and asked, "Are you wiping off my kiss?"

He paused, and thinking mighty fast replied, "No, Grandma, I'm rubbing it in."

Like this loving grandmother, God also kisses each of us in many different ways.

Do we hurry to rub it off? When it comes to God's love for us, do we duck his kiss because we do not want to be beholden to him?

We all want to be independent and make our own decisions. Do we think that if we accept God's loving kisses, it will obligate us to submit to his authority and conform our lives to his plans?

This is too hard for us, we fear, so we are tempted to turn away from God and his kisses.

A thousand times a day we may resist his kindness and block the channels of his life-giving love.

We brush off a helping hand or snub a friend.

We turn on the television or internet instead of turning to our families and friends.

We abandon our loved ones under the pretense that we need to "find ourselves" first.

We get high on drinking or drugs rather than getting high on life.

Why do we do this to ourselves?

We hurry past a poor beggar as he holds out his dirty hand for a coin.

We avert our eyes from an invalid in a wheelchair.

We close our doors to the downtrodden, and thereby miss the chance to entertain an angel.

Why do we make it so difficult to receive a kiss?

We ignore, even take for granted, the sun shining brightly overhead. We protest against God's authority. We may even leave our church and start a new one.

We disregard his loving commandments and treat them as mere suggestions.

We distain his righteous ways, dismiss his sacred Word and brush aside his grace-filled sacraments.

Finally, we lose the hospitality in our hearts, and our cheeks grow cold.

Why do we rub off his kisses in this manner?

Thank God, our Creator is persistent in seeking us! Our Prince of Peace yearns to awaken us from our lonely dream with his irresistible kiss of love.

If we accept the love of our Creator, we will be truly liberated. If we do not wipe away his kiss, we will discover that we are more inclined (and able) to do his will.

Far from being stifled or oppressed by his reign, as we feared, we rejoice to find ourselves unrestricted at last.

We are free to do his will, and we do it gladly because we know he seeks only our best when he kisses us.

Now we see ourselves clearly in the parable of the prodigal son: "while he was still a long way off, his father saw him and was filled with compassion for him; he ran to his son, threw his arms around him and kissed him" (Luke 15:20).

Gradually we discover a thousand of God's kisses coming our way every day.

Every smile that we receive and every kindness that we perceive is now recognized as a life-giving kiss from God.

We find faith, hope and love in unexpected places.

To our surprise, as often as we receive God's kisses we find ourselves inspired to offer similar charity to others.

With every helping hand we give, every sin that we forgive, and every life that we let live, we magnify his love and multiply his blessings.

So the next time God kisses your cheek, do not be so quick to rub it off…rather, rub it in.

Then turn the other cheek - for more kisses!

HEALING

*"Many followed Him,
and he healed them all."*

- St. Matthew

†

Painful memories
healed by Christ

When memories are painful, they may seem impossible to escape.

Sometimes they seem to haunt us like ghosts and taunt us with nightmares.

We all suffer from painful memories as a result of sin. We remember injuries, broken relationships, and deaths of loved ones. Life is filled with injustice, poverty, and war.

Since we live in a fallen and sinful world people inevitably hurt us, and we hurt others.

A bad memory can be like a deep splinter, depriving us of sleep, joy, and peace of mind. It can cause us to lose sight of the goodness in life, like the war veteran who watches a glorious sunset and grumbles "That looks like a bomb exploding."

Unpleasant thoughts can often be excruciating, like being hung on a wooden cross. Sometimes it can seem as if it is too much to bear.

Memories can cause us anxiety, plunge us into depression, and lead us "into the valley of the shadow of death." (Psalm 23) Life may seem gray and colorless. We may become confused, and mistake friends for enemies.

The fear of memories can make us angry and bitter, or drive us to seek solace in food, alcohol, drugs, pornography, sex, ultra-sports, gambling, or work.

Many of our ancestors in the Bible suffered from painful memories. Daniel recalled, "I was troubled in spirit, and the visions that passed through my mind disturbed me." (Daniel 7:14) Moses became delirious with anger, and killed an Egyptian. David's memories caused him to cry, "The cords of death entangled me, the anguish of the grave came upon me." (Psalms 116:3) Samson became so bitter in his mind that he shouted, "Since you acted like this, I will surely take revenge on you." (Judges 15) Judas was so tormented after betraying Jesus that he committed suicide.

The good news is that we can find wonderful healing for our painful memories.

We begin by turning to Jesus, who says "Come to me, all you who are heavy-burdened, and I will give you rest." (Matthew 11:28)

Next we may need to seek, receive or give genuine forgiveness to others. We may have to ask God to forgive us our trespasses, or forgive those who trespass against us. We may need to forgive God for allowing a painful experience in our lives. Sometimes hardest of all, we may need to forgive ourselves for past sins we have committed.

When we find comfort in forgiveness bright sunlight pierces the dark clouds, and we rejoice in our merciful God who promises, "I will remember their sins no more." (Hebrews 8:11)

If our aching memories persist, it may be God's way of getting our attention or to teach us an important lesson. God can use our painful memories to call us to a more intimate and prayerful relationship with him before he heals us.

God may also be calling us to use our painful memories in service to others, to comfort them, and perhaps in doing so, to help us find our own comfort.

Perhaps our Creator is also calling us to a deeper compassion for others and to become a wounded healer. We see this in the cancer survivor who volunteers at the hospital, the rape victim who counsels via hotline calls, the ex-convict who ministers in prison, and the amputee who visits disabled veterans.

In serving others we share profoundly in the life of Jesus, who used his pain to redeem our world.

Gradually we realize that while our painful memories are not yet fully erased in this life, we are given the healing grace and consolation to live with them supernaturally.

Imagine kneeling before Jesus, as he gently places his hands on your head and whispers, "Peace I leave with you; my peace I give to you. It's not as the world gives, but as I give to you" (John 14:27)

To repair your soul, call a Divine handyman

If we only knew how much our Lord wants to help us fix the problems in our lives, and how skillful he really is, we might turn to him sooner than we do.

We would gladly place ourselves completely in his loving hands.

To glimpse this approach to fixing everything, I recommend an entertaining television series called "This Old House".

It features a delightful cast of super-handy tradesmen who show up with all the right tools to fix everyday problems in ordinary homes.

They tackle every project with great confidence and enthusiasm, and after a while they usually uncover an unexpected problem caused by the homeowner's neglect or lack of knowledge.

A recent episode featured my favorite character, Norm Abram, an experienced carpenter with a red-checkered shirt, thick eyeglasses and big calloused hands.

As he carefully removed the siding from a house he discovered a long-hidden water leak that had seeped down from the roof, rotting the wood foundation of the home.

He showed the homeowner the problem and said, "This has to be fixed or it will ruin your whole house."

The homeowner appeared shocked by the revelation but was also glad to discover the source of the problem.

Relieved to be in the presence of a capable and honest repairman, the homeowner gratefully gave permission for him to proceed with fixing the problem.

When Norm was finished the house was repaired perfectly, and everyone was smiling.

This popular show appeals to me because it represents what Jesus wants to do for us. He wants to fix us up - completely. He wants to make us better than ever.

The Master Carpenter seeks to renew us, to fix us in our broken places and make us good as new.

He already knows exactly what needs fixing. "God is greater than our hearts, and he knows everything" (1 John 3:20).

He wants to unplug our stopped-up communications, repair our rusty relationships, restore the crumbling foundations of our lives and upgrade the circuits of our minds.

We know we are broken in some way, and we all need the healing hand of Christ. We need only call upon him. He will quickly go to work on us with infinite care and marvelous results.

Most of us know that we have a drippy habit needing transformation, a broken heart in need of mending, or a dark room in our soul requiring new light. However, we neglect it because we are afraid to investigate it alone.

We fear that the problem may be too big for us to solve, or we assume the problem has no solution.

Most daunting of all, we do not believe we know anyone honest or capable enough to fix the problem.

We need to realize that our Creator has all the answers.

We need to trust his promise that he has our best interests at heart. Then we can run to him with confidence.

We may have to wait awhile for him to finish his work, but he promises to make us perfect in his time. We just need to remember to allow him to proceed on his Divine schedule and not expect him to meet our impatient deadlines.

So let us call on the Master Craftsman to come fix us today. He is willing to help us; he is wanting to help us; and he is waiting to help us. All we need to do is ask.

Then we will hear an eager knock on our door and a reassuring voice saying, "I will build you up, and not tear you down" (Jeremiah 42:10).

†

God loves to heal a broken heart

An attractive woman arrived for our Bible Study in an expensive Mercedes.

As she stepped out of her car, I noticed her license plate spelled a provocative message: 2SXC4U.

Her striking beauty dazzled us but her words soon conveyed a deeper, more sobering message.

With tears in her eyes she said, "I have finally arrived at the point where I realize the only thing I have accomplished in my life is to make a complete mess. I do not want to live my way anymore; I want to live God's way."

Our hearts went out to her. Her enviable appearance and wealth suddenly seemed pitiful, having perhaps even contributed to her desolation. She was clearly relieved to be joining our group. Glad of our friendship, she gradually relaxed.

Our Lord welcomes us the same way. He invites us to give up our pride and lay down our heavy burdens. He seeks us, and calls us by name, and receives us in humility. He longs for us to return to him, and extends his loving hand.

However, we are stubborn and resist. We exult in doing things our way. We selfishly cling to our independence and remain defiant, shackled by our pride. Like Frank Sinatra, we relish singing "I Did It My Way."

When our hearts are hard, we resemble Pharaoh in the Book of Exodus, refusing to grant freedom for the Israelites to find the Promised Land. Our rock-hard hearts keep our souls captive, and we refuse to liberate our deepest longings to find God.

We hear "pride goes before destruction, and a haughty spirit before a fall." (Proverbs 16:18) Yet we continue to enslave ourselves with arrogance. When we imprison ourselves with conceit, we cause immense sadness to others and to God.

Why are we so smug? The truth is we want to be in control. We cling fiercely to pride, even though it makes us "weep in secret" (Jeremiah 13:17).

After many sorrows, we look in the mirror and discover that we have been living on our terms; not according to God's light.

We do not want to trust God because it means living his way. Therefore we strike out on our own, and stumble on the stones of selfishness.

On the other hand, if we allow ourselves to be still and listen quietly, we hear the whisper of a wonderful secret; "the Lord is close to the brokenhearted, and saves those who are crushed in spirit." (Psalm 34:18)

As we look more carefully, in the Bible and in our own experience, we learn with astonishment that God is seeking to heal us, and empower us, but he will only do so when we approach him in humility.

Then we realize why our pride grieves Jesus, because it precludes him from healing us and making us whole; "They would not see with their eyes and understand with their hearts, and turn to me so I could heal them." (John 12:40)

When we finally turn to Jesus, as an empty vessel seeking to be filled, we allow him to heal us in marvelous ways we cannot imagine.

So the next time you feel your heart breaking, let it break with gratitude. Abandon your bitterness, fear and resentment. Kneel in prayer, and expect to receive God's promise: "I will give you a new heart and put a new spirit in you; I will remove from you your heart of stone and give you a heart of flesh." (Ezekiel 36:26)

Ask Jesus to give you a heart like his; a humble heart, a servant's heart, a sacred heart.

Then feel his loving embrace as he enfolds you in his arms. Give praise as he heals your heart and makes it new. Rejoice as your new heart beats in unison with his, overflowing with love.

†

You can be
a new creation

If you feel stuck in the mud, burdened by your past, or desperate for a new life, you will be delighted to hear one of the most appealing promises our Lord ever made: "Whoever is in Christ is a new creation" (2 Cor. 5:17).

This is certainly one of His most exciting, and confusing, promises. It seems too good to be true.

In this human world, we often try to renew ourselves with new clothes, new cars, new houses, or new spouses. However, sadly we remain the same inside. We need a more radical change, deep down in our souls.

We need a super-natural change.

How can we change so completely that we become a new creation? We cannot do it ourselves; God re-creates us when we accept him as our Savior.

When we turn to Christ he runs toward us, welcoming us home with open arms. As in the parable of the prodigal son when the father runs to welcome his long-lost son, God forgives us all our sins as well. He unshackles us from our past and reconciles us with him. Thus renewed in love, we need not blush with shame in darkness and misery; instead, we may look upon God as he gazes upon us, radiant with joy.

So great is the change that God makes in our souls that we discover "the old things have passed away; behold, new things have come." (2 Cor 5:17) Our old thoughts and old habits pass away. God creates a new world in our souls, and all things are made new.

If you have difficulty believing this promise, or experiencing your new life, you are not alone. Pray for God's grace, or consider finding a friendly priest from whom to receive the gift of the Sacrament of Reconciliation.

Once we realize that we are indeed a new creation, what shall we do with our new life?

God has divinely commissioned us to go out into the world and proclaim the good news of Jesus Christ.

On his behalf, he wants us to help him create his Kingdom here on Earth. He wants us to co-operate with him.

As a child helps his father fix something which is broken, so also we can help our heavenly father fix this world.

As present-day disciples, we can assist in bringing God's glorious desire to fruition by reconciling all people to him and to each other. Truly, our new life in Christ is a great privilege and an awesome responsibility.

"We are ambassadors for Christ," Paul says, "as if God were appealing through us." Because we are now in Christ, we can be messengers of God.

He enables us to re-present him, speaking and acting on his behalf. Transformed beyond our wildest dreams, we can speak Christ's words of reconciliation to everyone.

In spite of almost-certain rejection, we must reach out to others to bandage and heal them, comfort and appeal to them: "We implore you, on behalf of Christ, be reconciled to God." (2 Cor 5:20)

Above all, we proclaim the good news to others so that they may discover the deepest desire of all human hearts. Thus do we find ourselves continuing the work of Christ, gently turning hearts and minds to God. He welcomes everyone, reconciles all souls in harmony, and re-creates them in his image and likeness.

Therefore we labor in humility to make his good news known to all people. If we work diligently and listen carefully, we will hear the voice of God whispering in our ear, at an unexpected hour, "Behold, I make all things new."

†

Unborn babies jumping for joy

John the Baptist is one of my favorite people in the Bible. When he was still an infant in Elizabeth's womb, he "leapt for joy" when his mother met Mary, who was pregnant with Jesus.

Today we might imagine all babies jumping for joy over the U.S. Supreme Court decision to better protect life in the womb.

In a decision of historic consequences, the Supreme Court recently prohibited partial-birth abortion, a gruesome and horrifying procedure which partially delivers a living fetus and then kills it.

The decision is a significant victory in the ongoing battle to protect and defend the most innocent and helpless members of our human family: our unborn children.

The vote was five votes in favor; four opposed. All votes in favor came from the Justices who are Catholic.

A friend of mine heard the news and exclaimed "Halleluiah! Now that they've made partial-birth abortion illegal maybe they'll make all abortion illegal."

She was referring, of course, to the infamous Roe vs. Wade decision handed down by the Supreme Court in 1973 legalizing abortion; a regrettable decision that has resulted in the deaths of over 45 million unborn children in the U.S to date.

To see this in perspective, abortion has resulted in more deaths than all the wars, murders, famines, crimes and plagues in the past 300 years of human history.

Predictably, those who favor death are now howling to protest this decision, as a deadly lion roars in rage when its prey is snatched from its jaws.

Make no mistake; this is a battle with fierce opposition.

A mother's womb is made by God to be the ultimate safe harbor, the most sacred repository of new life. Yet a womb is still the most dangerous place to live in America. Forget the news reports about the biggest killers being smoking, heart disease or accidents; by far the biggest killer is abortion.

My heart grieves for the millions of children forsaken by their mothers and by pride. Their fruitful lives are cast aside, and their potential brides and grooms are utterly denied.

I pray especially, as we all do, for hurting mothers and fathers who may still mourn, and hope that they find the comfort, consolation and peace of Christ. He is the one who offers grace, forgiveness and new life to all who believe in him.

Surely this is the seminal issue of our time, as slavery was the greatest issue faced by a previous generation.

I predict that in our lifetime we will see abortion outlawed, just as an enlightened Supreme Court outlawed slavery in an earlier era.

Recently I saw the movie "Amazing Grace," which showed how the slave trade was eliminated in England in the 1700's thanks to the heroic efforts of William Wilberforce.

Someday I hope that we, as a society, will look back on abortion just as we remember the now-forbidden slave trade; as a distant memory of a more barbaric, less-civilized time.

One factor that helps in stopping abortions is the ultrasound machine. When pregnant mothers can see the shape and form of their unborn children, they are more likely to awaken to the wonderful and unmistakable miracle of new life hidden inside them.

In the meantime a formidable battlefield stands before us, calling us to summon our heroes to the front. We must stride forth valiantly, with virtue and righteousness on our side. We are armed with faith, brimming with hope, and pouring out love with which to vanquish the powers and principalities of darkness. As did Jesus, one heart at a time.

Let us remember how Mary and Elizabeth, pregnant with Jesus and John the Baptist, followed our Lord's wise counsel; "I have set before you life and death, the blessing and the curse. Choose life, that you and your descendants may live." (Deuteronomy 30:19)

†

First broken, then blessed

One morning at breakfast a farmer said he felt like a window.

When asked why the old man smiled and replied, "Full of panes, full of panes."

Sometimes we feel like that old farmer. Life can be a pain!

It hurts when we fall and scrape a knee or accidentally hit a thumb with a hammer.

More seriously, we may suffer a painful medical condition, a jagged-edged experience, or a broken relationship.

Life can break our hearts and shatter our dreams. We may fear it is impossible to put the pieces of our lives back together again.

In the midst of our suffering and brokenness, we may recall that our King allowed himself to be broken and crucified.

His fear caused him to sweat drops of blood, and he pleaded with God by saying, "let this cup pass from me".

Yet Jesus, in humility, allowed himself to be broken. Why did he endure this? Because he trusted his Father's promise that on the third day he would rise again to be with Him in heaven.

We can trust God the same way. Whenever God allows us to be broken, we believe that he promises to bless us with new life.

The Master Craftsman wants us to turn toward him so he can rebuild us better than ever, in his image and likeness.

First we are broken, and then we are blessed.

Our faith does not take away pain. Faith instills pain with consecrated meaning and gives us supernatural hope.

"Offer it up," my grandfather would say about sufferings both great and small.

Do it now. By resting in God's hands, you will find new courage, greater strength, and unexpected peace in the midst of distress.

A young woman I know was diagnosed with a frightening type of cancer. Her doctor arrived with a solemn face and announced, "I'm afraid I have some bad news."

With a serene smile she responded, "Oh, Doctor, you don't have to worry about me. I'm a Christian."

She believed deep down that our Creator's blessings are contained in every situation, giving her "the peace of God that surpasses understanding" (Phil. 4:7).

Jesus demonstrated and embodied this mystery of brokenness during the Last Supper. He took the bread, broke it, blessed it, and said, "Take this, all of you, and eat it. This is my body, which will be given up for you."

Jesus was soon broken on the cross, and then God blessed him.

In the same way, when we are broken God will bless us, too.

Just when we fear we can no longer bear our pain, the darkness that overshadows our brokenness is penetrated by a great light, and all our troubles melt away with the rising sun of a new day.

Therefore, instead of fearing our brokenness as an enemy, we may embrace it as a friend. Just as we bless our enemies, we may also bless our pains and heartbreaks, trusting they are blessings in disguise.

We do not enjoy suffering, yet we can accept it gracefully when it comes. We know God allows it as a prelude to blessing us beyond our imagination.

While our suffering is a great mystery, God promises to put us back together again. This is our faith and hope.

Our darkness is temporary. Love and laughter will return, often in the midst of the darkness, multiplied like loaves and fishes.

Remember the disciples who despaired after Jesus was crucified? When he reappeared, they did not recognize him. During supper, Jesus again broke the bread and blessed it. "With that their eyes were opened and they recognized him" (Luke 24:30).

First we are broken, and then we are blessed. Then our eyes are opened, and we see God.

HOPING

*"Be strong and let
your heart take courage,
all you who hope in the Lord."*

- Psalm 31

Rejoice in darkness before the dawn

Sometimes life seems dark and spooky, especially in the middle of the night when it seems everyone is fast asleep but you.

Everything may be sailing along smoothly, then suddenly something happens that hurts us or someone we love, and this can plunge us into darkness and despair.

It may come in the form of a phone call, a doctor's visit, or a letter. It may be the loss of your health or wealth. It may be the loss of a friend, family member, or spouse. It may be the loss of your faith, hope, or love.

Suddenly everything seems strange, desolate, uncertain.

As in a nightmare, your hopes and dreams may seem far away or impossible. Life can break your heart so much it takes your breath away. It may feel frightening, like drowning, suffocating, or falling into a deep well.

The darkness itself is terrifying.

Now is the time to call upon your Comforter. Look up, and see the face of God. See him looking down at you from on high, his face shining and smiling. Now see him sitting next to you, putting his arm around you. He is listening. Now is the time to talk to him. Tell him your fears, pour out your tears.

Ask him to comfort you, heal you, and guide you through this dark night of your soul.

Listen as he speaks to you, telling you to fear not, be anxious for nothing, for he is with you all the days of your life. Let him quietly explain that he understands and that he is with you every step of the way.

You may protest that you hurt too much, and that you do not understand why this is happening.

Hear him reply that he will never allow you to suffer more than you are able, and that you need not understand what is happening; you need only trust him. He knows. He cares. He holds you in his hands.

Call him Counselor, Great Physician, Peace Giver, Joy Bringer, Forgiver, Reconciler, Love Finder, Life Changer, Faithful Friend, and "Abba" Father.

Relax now, as he describes how he created the universe long ago, the heavens and earth, light and darkness, plants and birds and animals, and our original parents. It was all good.

Then sin entered the world, because of disobedience, so he sent his only son Jesus to die for us and for our sins, to redeem the world and reopen the doors of heaven.

For the present, we walk as pilgrims, seeing only the backside of the tapestry of life. It is only when we reach the other side that we will see clearly the magnificent design that he has been creating all along.

Listen as he proclaims, "I am the light of the world; he who follows me will not walk in the darkness, but will have the light of life." (John 8:12)

You may question how this is possible, since the present seems so bleak. He replies, "I will lead the blind by a way they do not know, in paths they do not know, I will guide them. I will make darkness into light before them, and rugged places into plains." (Isaiah 42:16)

He gently reminds you that he promises, in his timing, to give you peace, rest, comfort, guidance, healing, perfect health, love, wisdom, a land flowing with milk and honey, the kingdom of heaven, and eternal life.

He continues; "You will surely forget your trouble, recalling it only as waters gone by. Life will be brighter than noonday, and darkness will become like morning." (Job 11:16)

Now you can rest easy, and rejoice before the dawn.

†

Behold, your dream
has come true

A little girl in pajamas kneeled for bedtime prayers; "Dear God, thank you for the baby brother, but what I really wanted was a puppy."

We all want something special, that is for sure.

As babies we cry for milk, warmth or a loving touch. As children we want toys, sweets and love. As adults we want meaningful work, health and wealth. We always long for what we do not possess, and pray for our heartfelt desires.

On a deeper level we seek freedom from our limitations: fear, pride, addictions, psychological and emotional pain.

Our desolation is essentially spiritual, caused by our sins and the sins of others. We need forgiveness, reconciliation, renewal, and consolation.

We may not know it, but on the deepest level our souls are really seeking God. "Our hearts are restless, until they find their rest in God," said St. Augustine.

In this, we resemble our ancestors in Old Testament times who earnestly awaited the Promised One. They longed for a messiah, foretold by the prophets and promised many times in Holy Scripture. For centuries people waited in expectation; including shepherds in their fields, weavers at their looms, and carpenters at their benches.

Families gathered in the evenings around simple food, illuminated only by flickering candlelight or a small sparking fire. They raised their eyes to heaven and prayed for the coming of their Savior.

They expected a rich and powerful man to rise up and conquer their enemies; to liberate them from their oppressors; and to deliver them into wealth, power, and prestige.

Then one day the messiah was actually born! Word traveled slowly, by foot or camel, from Bethlehem throughout the ancient world.

Imagine their excitement upon hearing that the messiah was born. Think of their amazement, the joy and jubilation! The long-awaited time had arrived; their hopes and dreams were realized at last!

Imagine also their confusion and perplexity upon hearing that the messiah had been born in a cold, smelly stable to parents of such low estate. Some may have thought, "How can this be? We were expecting a prince, or a king, born in a noble palace!" They may have felt discouraged, until later events proved him glorious beyond their comprehension.

Today our hopes and dreams come true the same way; at unexpected times, shrouded in quiet humility. The answer to our prayers may appear so little, so disguised or obscure that it escapes our attention or admiration.

In fact, the fulfillment we seek may already have arrived, unnoticed. Like the birth of the Christ-child two thousand years ago, our hopes and dreams may have already been fulfilled.

Our salvation is often not sufficiently attractive, rich or exalted enough to suit us. The true beauty and meaning of our destiny may be hidden behind a veil of illness, adversity, or hardship. We may overlook the child, person, or event sent by God as the answer to our most ardent desires.

If we quiet ourselves, and turn our gaze toward heaven, we see more clearly. We realize that we have already received our blessings, just not as we expected. Since God is the creator of the universe, and also gave us His Son, we realize with astonishment that we already have everything we need and more than we can imagine.

Now we discover the miracle of new life every day. Like shepherds in the field, we hear the voice of an angel saying, "Behold, I proclaim to you good news of great joy that will be for all the people. For today in the City of David, a Savior has been born for you." (Luke 2:10)

Your best gift
is waiting for you

When the days get cold in winter, and the snow comes fluttering down, I remember my parents gathering all of us children around a roaring fire in the living room for an evening of enchantment.

As we roasted marshmallows, sang carols and sipped hot cocoa, the glowing fire warmed our bodies and souls. The flickering flames made our cheeks and lips rosy, our noses toasty and our dogs cozy.

With little fingers, we each wrote on a tiny piece of tissue paper what we wanted for Christmas. Gently we draped each tissue on the metal poker, held it above the fire, watched it fly up the chimney with the sparks, and disappear.

Sometimes the delicate tissue caught fire and burned our heartfelt messages to ashes. Then we had to start over and try again.

I found it quite mysterious as to how my message flew all the way to the North Pole where Santa read it personally.

One year, using my best handwriting, I earnestly scrawled "a purple bike".

As Christmas drew near our anticipation grew, and we looked forward to rushing downstairs to see how Santa had granted our wishes.

My father always put up a white bed sheet to block the entrance to the living room and said to us "No peeking!"

We squirmed, begged, and pleaded for him to hurry and take it down. He pretended to take his time, a ploy designed to increase our appreciation.

When he asked, "Are you ready?" we all jumped up and down yelling, "Yes!" He repeated, "Are you sure you're ready?" We all screamed louder, "YES!"

Just when we were ready to explode with excitement, our father removed the sheet and we burst into the living room to behold our gifts in front of a crackling fire.

The year I asked for a purple bicycle I scanned my gifts, but it was nowhere in sight. Deflated, I resigned myself to receiving another gift.

After everyone had opened their presents my father said to me, "Close your eyes." His words enraptured me as I waited with mounting hope. At last he announced, "You can open your eyes now."

And there it stood: a purple bike with a headlight. I felt like the happiest kid in the world that day.

Grown-ups have a tendency to lose this youthful exuberance and joyful anticipation. Perhaps they did not get the gift they wanted, or the life they expected, so they become disillusioned. They think God does not care.

We all need to remember Jesus' promise; "Everyone who asks receives; and the one who seeks, finds." Jesus gives us hope; "If you...know how to give good gifts to your children, how much more will your heavenly Father give good things to those who ask him." (Matthew 7: 8)

Since you know God will give you good things, expect his good gifts with the open heart of a child. Like young St. Therese, the "Little Flower", you can live with complete confidence and trust in his love.

Ask for faith and hope, and then get ready for the great Gift Giver to appear. Start looking up the chimney with wonder, and gaze up into the sky "to see if reindeer really know how to fly."

You will naturally begin to laugh easier and sleep better. Expect to dream of dancing sugarplums, a baby in a hay manger, and an old man with a white beard giving gifts to many children.

In an unexpected hour, past midnight, when you love the Lord with all your heart and all your soul and all your strength, when you are ready to burst with unfulfilled desire, your heavenly Father will remove your veil of doubt and say; "You can open your eyes now."

✝
Spiritual exercise
is good for your soul

"My life has changed," said my friend.

She spoke with excitement and a big smile.

"Since I discovered the power of gratitude, I see everything and everyone in a new light. I no longer see the glass half-empty; now I see the glass half-full."

This woman had struggled with a critical spirit, as well as a self-proclaimed tendency to see a problem in every situation and a fault in every person.

She also worried that her kids were copying her bad habits.

Then she read *The Spiritual Exercises of Saint Ignatius* and discovered the power of gratitude.

On the first page Ignatius stirred her heart with these words: "Man is created to praise, reverence, and serve God our Lord."

As she practiced the spiritual exercises of Saint Ignatius, she found herself allowing God to guide her to supernatural health. She had found a new personal trainer.

During her nightly examination of conscience, she reflected on her day. Then she thanked God for all his blessings, and praised him for his own sake.

"I discovered," she recalled, "how to put myself entirely in God's loving hands and praise him for all things. Nothing good or bad happens unless God allows it to pass through his fingers. So we can be grateful for everything."

"My life is transformed," she continued. "I feel like I've awakened from a delirious nightmare. Maybe I found the Holy Spirit. I just want to share this joy and wisdom with the world!"

She decided to offer her children an easy version of the spiritual exercises by asking them three questions.

Now every night at bedtime, starting with the youngest, she sits on the side of the bed as they kneel and say their prayers.

She listens intently to them, just as God listened to her.

Then they jump into bed and she tucks them in saying, "Name one thing you are thankful for."

At first, she recalled, they mentioned ice cream, flowers and birthday parties. Gradually they expanded their lists to include surprises like grandpa's laugh or a teacher's compliment.

This helps her children see the endless variety of God's blessings every day.

Previously they rocketed through the day without noticing God's blessings. Now they notice more blessings, and it shows in their radiant faces.

Next she asks, "What is one thing you might have done differently today?"

This teaches them how to be more aware of their words and actions. They learn to be problem solvers and peacemakers. They dream of creative ways to be better in the future.

Finally she says, "Name one time today when you felt God's presence."

This helps them recognize God's loving presence in their daily lives. In little ways and in big ways. In the beauty of nature and the warmth of the sun. In the people they meet and the friendships they make.

Her older children are starting to appreciate how God can bring good from bad and healing after hurt.

This gently moves them closer to God by helping them identify his certain presence every day of their lives.

Gradually they see God in all the love they give and receive, for God *is* love.

Then the children drift off to sleep knowing the peace and joy of the Great Comforter.

"This nightly ritual," she says, "is giving them a much deeper faith than I had as a child. I actually see my children now as little Saints in progress."

"I'm also starting," she adds, "to offer these same three questions to my husband, my nieces and nephews, and my students in Sunday School. They like the exercise and I enjoy helping God change their consciousness a little bit at a time."

The son who broke
his mother's heart

I'm here to tell you that he was a real troublemaker.

I personally saw him cause a lot of problems. He also broke his mother's heart, and that was the saddest thing I've ever seen.

It's no surprise, if you ask me, because no one knows his real father. If the kid was illegitimate and never knew his own father, what do you expect in such a careless and irresponsible situation?

Anyway, the punk showed his true colors early when he ran away from home. His mother and stepfather were frantic.

Turns out, he had walked into a nearby church and started a huge argument. Can you believe that? When his parents came to find him, worried as can be, he just scoffed at them. A bad attitude, just like a juvenile delinquent, if you ask me.

Then he went through a quiet phase for a while, helping his stepfather in his woodworking business. Everyone thought he was turning into a decent person.

But then one day he disappeared again and turned up with his cousin, a homeless bum who lived out in the country. Since his cousin was half-crazy, everyone knew trouble was afoot. That's when he really turned bad.

He began hanging out with the worst people in town, including prostitutes and crooked financiers, low-life individuals of questionable reputation, and invalids with incurable diseases. For some perverse reason, he sought out the worst outcasts in society and reveled in their repulsive company.

Gradually his flunkies became a dangerous gang. He started performing cult practices, including satanic rites and superstitious exorcisms. Soon there were dark rumors of cannibalism and human sacrifice, ritualistic ceremonies involving the consumption of human blood, and occult practices too outrageous for me to mention.

We know he struggled with personal demons because he spoke often of hearing voices and meeting devils. He even claimed supernatural power by invoking unearthly spirits.

Once he went mad with rage, violently assaulting a group of ordinary people in a church and physically throwing them out.

Soon the respectable members of society wanted nothing to do with him. Can you blame them?

In my opinion, he was narcissistic, manic-depressive, antisocial, pathological, psychotic, schizophrenic, and utterly out of touch with reality. Some believe he had a messiah complex with delusions of grandeur. He must have been full of sorrow because he acted as if he had a death wish.

Well the police finally caught up with him. One of his hooligans claimed a cash reward and turned him in.

Near the end, he cut off all ties with his family and publicly rebuked his mother. You could see that really broke her heart. She was crying, "I can't live without him."

On his court date, he refused repeated opportunities to maintain his innocence, so of course he was sentenced for his nefarious crimes.

Popular opinion probably helped convict him, as the public outcry over the heinousness of his crimes reached a fever pitch.

In any case, as a testament to the rightness of his sentence, the bloodthirsty crowd went wild with delight and created a near-riot, chanting "Execute him, execute him!" It sends a cold chill up my spine just thinking about it. I can't say I blame them, given the amount of trouble he caused during his short and miserable life.

Unfortunately, they botched the execution, and it took a while to put him out of his misery. Anyway, it's a darn shame, but what did he expect after causing all that trouble? He caused division and controversy everywhere he went.

Well that's all I've got to say, I've had too much to drink and I've got to hurry home to the wife. Mrs. Pilate will wonder where I've been, and the weather has been getting steadily worse all afternoon.

In fact, I've never seen it so dark…

In all hardship find God's love

Ronald Reagan's favorite joke featured a little boy whose parents worried that their son was just too optimistic. So they took him to see a psychiatrist.

Trying to dampen the boy's spirits, the psychiatrist showed him into a room piled high with nothing but horse manure.

The little boy jumped on top of the pile and began gleefully digging with his bare hands.

"What are you doing?" the psychiatrist asked.

"With all this manure," the little boy exclaimed, "there must be a pony in here somewhere!"

Like this little boy, we can choose how we will respond to life's misfortunes. Everyone experiences rejection, disappointment, failure, and heartache. It is easy to become negative, to see the cup half empty, instead of half full. But if we exercise the gift of faith, we seek God's love and find hope.

Throughout Scripture, our Creator promises us that he seeks our best. Isn't that wonderful? He cares about us so much. If you seek out the best in all things, including your sorrows and misfortunes, you are seeking His way.

God always transforms all of our hardships into blessings. He wants us to come to him. "God causes all things to work together for good." (Romans 8:28)

God makes everything turn out for the best. Always.

Your distress today may be serious: a lost job, an accident or injury, or a health scare. You may be suffering from a betrayal, an addiction, a marriage crisis, or financial failure.

Be optimistic, and lean on God. Expect a good outcome. Start digging.

Ready to try it now? Whatever is causing you pain or suffering today, instead of wallowing in fear or misery, think how it can become a blessing.

Sick or injured? Catch up on prayer and reading. Lost your job? You are liberated to find a better job. Difficult relationship? Try to become more loving. Family member causing trouble? Learn more about forgiveness.

Make up an impossibly far-fetched, but favorable, outcome. Like a writer who rescues his hero or heroine from certain death, you may choose any happy ending you wish.

That is fine to do, you say, but what about catastrophic events? What if we are plunged into total darkness and shaken to the core?

We may feel overwhelmed by permanent loss of health or chronic pain. We may be stripped of our ability to imagine a good outcome to a failed marriage or the death of a loved one.

When we no longer have strength in ourselves, we must turn to God as our only hope. Like Jesus on the cross, we can surrender ourselves completely into God's hands. It is precisely at this moment that we find God. In our extreme suffering, we find that God is our pony.

Whatever your hardship today, no matter how discouraged you feel, rejoice in knowing that God is using your suffering right now in your favor. You may not be able to see how he is doing it. Just believe His promise that he is redeeming your situation in hidden and marvelous ways.

Try to pray, "Thank you for my cross, Jesus, now show me the way." Believe the words, enter into the words, and live your faith with all your mind, body and soul. When you do this you become like Jesus; a living embodiment of the word of our Lord. You are alive in Christ, sharing His joyful destiny.

So the next time life buries you in problems, think to yourself, "There must be a pony in here somewhere!" and start digging.

You may not find the pony you expect, but you will certainly find God.

LOVING

"Faith, hope, love,
abide these three;
but the greatest of these is love."

- St. Paul

Do you speak
the language of love?

A recent television program showed a young couple engaged in a heated argument.

They stood nose to nose and screamed at each another.

The host of the show incited them to heightened displays of anger while the studio audience roared their approval.

Clearly these people were not speaking the language of love.

If you have difficulty communicating with a key person in your life, chances are you are not speaking his or her language of love.

Each of us is born with a preference for a specific love language, as described by Dr. Gary Chapman in his bestselling book *The Five Love Languages* (Northfield Publishing).

The result of his 30 year experience as a marriage counselor, this four-million-copy blockbuster identifies five love languages: Words of Affirmation, Quality Time, Receiving Gifts, Acts of Service, and Physical Touch.

Some people crave focused attention; others need regular praise. Gifts are highly important to some, while another sees cooking a meal as an act of love. Some people find physical touch makes them feel valued.

Mark Twain once said, "I can live for two months on a good compliment." Can you guess his love language?

Most of us are so keen to receive love in our special language that its absence makes us feel unloved or incapable of responding to the other person.

We may even be so "tuned in" to our special dialect of love that we are unaware of the fact that others have a completely different language. We end up shouting at them in our own dialect and wondering why they fail to understand us or respond to us.

Their inability to communicate with us may seem careless and loveless. We may be tempted to see them as evil.

We need to realize that the other person simply does not speak our love language. We might as well be trying to communicate with someone from China. They simply do not understand us, nor do we understand them.

The key is to learn their love language.

Do you know the love language of the people nearest to you? Your spouse, children, parents and friends? How about your boss, co-workers, and neighbors?

How do you learn their love language? Simply observe and listen to them. Most people communicate their love in the way they most need to receive it themselves.

If you are still unsure, just ask. Most people are delighted to tell you their preferred love language.

Fortunately, we have a loving God who teaches us how to speak the different languages of love. The Great Communicator sent his son Jesus to be our role model.

I admire how Jesus communicated love perfectly to each person he met. Here's how Jesus demonstrated the five love languages:

"The Son of Man did not come to be served but to serve" (Mark 10:45).

"He spent some time with them" (John 3:22).

"He touched her hand" (Matthew 8:15).

"This is my body, which will be given for you" (Luke 22:19).

"Well done, my good and faithful servant" (Matthew 25:21).

If you truly take time to learn another person's love language, you may be amazed at how quickly you come to appreciate each other. Long-locked doors of communication may open; the light of understanding may illuminate your relationship. Divine intimacy may be yours.

Now the journey is yours to enjoy as you discover the endless variety of ways to touch, compliment, serve, give gifts to and spend time with your beloved.

In this way you become like St. Francis, who said, "Seek not so much to be understood as to understand, to be loved as to love."

Do not despair; love is everywhere

Sitting in her favorite chair by a sunny window in the convent, a young nun opened her stack of mail.

One of the letters was a birthday card from her brother with a gift of $80 in cash.

Of course the sister had no use for the money, since she had taken a vow of poverty. As she was contemplating what to do with it, she noticed a homeless man sitting on the curb outside.

She opened the window and handed the money to the man saying, "Don't despair."

The next day the man returned with $8,000 for the sister. When she asked where he had gotten the money, he excitedly told her "Don't Despair came in at 100 to one!"

Like the nun in this joke, we can be surprised when we share our gift of love.

We can never be sure what people will do with it, and we never know how or when it will come back to us.

On a deeper level, I am awestruck when I consider that all love originates with God. My ability to love comes from him. God originates all love; it starts with him. He loves me first; and this enables me to love him in return, and to love others.

This is true for all of us; our ability to love is enabled by God's love of us. "We love, because he first loved us." (1 John 4:19)

What will we do with his gift?

Will we gamble with it, or squander it? Better yet, will we plant it deep in our souls, and cultivate it as a priceless seed so that it increases a hundredfold?

When we share God's love with other people, this enables them to experience his love. It inspires them to return that same love, to God and to others.

Sometimes, sadly, others may not reciprocate.

We all know people in our lives who we love but who are thankless, poor in spirit, or spiritually homeless. They do not return our love.

They may be squandering our love, and we do not know if they will ever return it. They may be gambling with our love, or learning how to appreciate it somewhere else, maybe with someone else. We may never see them again, and in the meantime our love is unrequited.

Yet we need not despair. We may be hopeful that in God's good time, and if it is his will, they will return our love.

In the meantime, we may fortify and console ourselves by practicing the virtue of hope. We hope, by praying, that the seeds of love we spread will fall on fertile soil and produce a harvest.

To increase our hope, we can meditate on the parable of the sower, as told by Jesus: "...other seeds fell into the good soil, and yielded a crop, and produced thirty, sixty, and a hundredfold." (Mark 4:8)

We do well to remember that the seeds of love we sow must be selfless, self-giving, and sacrificial. This is true love; it requires us to give up our desires, maybe even a loved one, for God's sake.

After we have given up everything in love we may receive our reward a hundredfold, at an unexpected hour.

As Jesus promised, "Truly I say to you, there is no one who has left house or brothers or sisters or mother or father or children or farms, for My sake and for the gospel's sake, but they will receive a hundred times as much now in the present age... and in the age to come, eternal life." (Mark 10:29)

Marriage is like a bicycle built for two

High in the Sierra Mountains of California, I drove past a couple riding a bicycle built for two.

Huffing and puffing, straining in unison, they rode uphill with delight. They were obviously a good team.

Near the summit, they turned into a parking lot and dismounted.

Their cheeks were flushed red and their faces glistened in the sunlight, full of good health and fresh air.

"How far have you been biking?" I shouted.

"Sixty five miles," said the man proudly.

"You're kidding!" I replied. "You came across Death Valley?"

"Yes, it was great!" he exclaimed.

"Terrific!" she agreed.

Later that night we happened to meet in a restaurant, and they said they were married.

"Wouldn't it be easier on your marriage," I asked, "if you rode separate bikes?"

They both laughed and recalled that the man who made their custom bike said, "I hope you have a strong marriage!"

Again, I asked why they rode a tandem bike instead of individual bikes.

"Because it's easier to talk," he explained. "It's also better when one of us is having a bad day because the other person can give a burst of energy."

"Absolutely," she concurred. "If one of us is weak, the other is strong. Riding together evens us out."

It occurred to me that she was reiterating what St. Paul said 2,000 years ago, "Two are better than one. If the one falls, the other will lift up the companion. Where one person may be overcome, two together can succeed." (Ecclesiastes 4:9)

She continued: "It takes a lot of trust and working together, because I can't steer and I don't have any brakes. He controls them. I just pedal as hard as I can and help us keep our balance."

"The first trip we ever took on our tandem bike was down the entire Oregon coast," he said.
"It was tough, mentally and physically. We almost threw in the towel. We burned away all the fat we had!"

"He's tall and I'm short," she explained, "and I was not really a biker type."

He looked at her and smiled broadly, "You sure have become one."

I inquired of them if they ever argued.

"Sometimes," she replied. "I tap him on the back and say, 'We're going too fast!' But mostly we help each other, so if I am faltering, he will see me through, and vice versa. We talk to each other, y' know?"

He recalled that their marriage has not always been so harmonious. "When we were first married, we both had jobs and incomes. We sort of went our separate ways. Looking back on it, we did not work well together. Then we experienced many difficulties. Health and money and family problems forced us to grow together or apart – we chose together. Now we rely on each other all the time, because we work better working together."

As I left this adventurous couple, I glanced over my shoulder and saw them laughing and offering spoonfulls of ice cream to each other with delight.

They are a beautiful example of spouses who have learned by painful experience how to cooperate with love, not compete with pride.

Unknowingly, they had also given me a glimpse of our relationship with Jesus, who often describes himself as our Spouse. He is our Bridegroom, and we are his Bride. Imagine riding a tandem bike with Jesus steering in front of you. Would you worry where you were going, or how fast?

Next time you want to get closer to your spouse, or to Jesus, imagine riding a bicycle built for two. By cooperating with love, you will get farther, communicate better, and enjoy it more.

Love people first, then teach them

If you know someone who is difficult to reach, teach, or talk to, this true story is for you.

I had the good fortune recently to be seated at dinner next to a popular and beloved old priest.

Digging for gold, I asked him about his early years.

"My first job," he replied, "was teaching high school. I hated the noise and confusion. But once I discovered the secret of teaching, I loved it."

I looked up from my salad and asked, "What is the secret?"

He smiled and said, "I discovered that once my students realized I loved them, I could teach them anything."

That discovery, he explained, was the most valuable lesson in his life; better than anything he learned in seminary, and the secret to his success and joy as a priest.

As dinner ended, I thanked him wholeheartedly.

Driving home that night, I pondered his words in amazement. This is not the way of the world, I thought, this is the wisdom of Jesus.

This is how we are taught by the Greatest Teacher Who Ever Lived. He loves us first, and then later He teaches us.

A kind woman who runs a popular daycare program voices the same wisdom. When asked how she does it, she says, "I just show all the children how much I love them; then we get along just fine."

Our human nature is fallen and rebellious. Stubborn as mules, we need to be convinced and won over before we open our minds and hearts and get moving.

Lifeless as Adam on the ceiling of the Sistine Chapel in the Vatican, we need God to reach out and touch us into life.

Each of us needs the love of God to awaken us from darkness and give us life.

In other words, we are able to love and learn only after we are first loved by God. As Saint John says, "We love because he first loved us." (1 John 4:19)

I remember how difficult it was for me when I first started teaching and how easy it became when I realized I was not the most important person in the classroom.

My students taught me an invaluable lesson: that it is not about me. The message from each student was loud and clear: "I don't care how much you know -- until I know how much you care."

My friend who is a longtime third-grade teacher confirms this. He says, "No one believes the message until they believe in the messenger."

If someone in your life is difficult to teach, perhaps you need to show that person your love for him/her.

"There can be no rules without relationship," declares John McDowell, the premier speaker to teenagers across the United States.

Great minds think alike, don't they? The best teachers, coaches, parents and friends all practice this wisdom.

First, we must earn the respect and trust of others by ministering to them and their families. Only then can we bring up the lesson we wish to teach.

King David, one of the wisest men who ever lived, became a student of God by first pleading "Let me hear your loving kindness in the morning." Later he said, "I trust you. Teach me the way in which I should walk; for to You I lift up my soul." (Psalm 143:8)

David needed to feel he was receiving God's love before he could trust him.

When the crowd asked Jesus "What is the greatest commandment?" Jesus emphasized love. "Love the Lord your God with all your heart and with all your soul and with all your strength and with all your mind'; and, 'Love your neighbor as yourself.' " (Luke 10:27)

So the next time you want to get your point across to somebody, do it like Jesus: love first, teach later.

†

Human life begins before conception

A friend of mine is a surgeon who specializes in operating on babies before they are born.

Using a powerful microscope and ultra-fine surgical instruments, this gifted man performs precise life-saving techniques on babies while they are still in their mothers' wombs.

He is one of the most focused, careful and confident individuals I have ever known. To be sure, he operates in a realm previously unimaginable, a hidden domain filled with great beauty and mystery.

Throughout human history, a fierce battle has raged over this sacred ground of a woman's womb to determine when human life begins.

Science has recently answered this question conclusively: modern biology provides clear evidence that individual human life begins with the union of egg and sperm cell.

From the moment of fertilization, the cells are alive and producing a human being.

In other words, human life begins at conception. This is a proven scientific fact.

But wait; there is more to this story...

Our Lord informs us that each of us existed in a special way *before* we were born. Even before we were conceived by our biological mother and father, God conceived us supernaturally in his mind; "Before I formed you in the womb I knew you, and before you were born I consecrated you" (Jeremiah 1:5).

In the mind of God, human life begins before conception.

God wills, anticipates and intends the conception of each one of us. In some mysterious and marvelous way, since we exist in God's eternal mind before our conception, some aspect of our identity pre-existed our conception.

King David proclaimed, "All the days ordained for me were written in your book before one of them came to be." (Psalm 139:16)

As creatures, we begin our earthly lives at a unique and miraculous moment of fertilization that occurs in an unrepeatable moment in time.

Nevertheless, we retain an eternal dimension of our existence because we existed in the mind of God before we were conceived.

Thus, we each embody a spark of the Divine essence. Since God knows us and willed our existence before time began, this knowledge may inform and transform us.

We each inherit the priceless gift of a timeless history and eternal destiny that germinates, propagates, and illuminates our lives.

While we are merely pilgrims travelling this earth for a short time, yet we have an infinite radiance to our being here and now.

Even more marvelously, God tells us in Genesis that he creates each one of us in his image. The knowledge that we reflect God's holy imprint and heavenly expression is humbling, breathtaking and exhilarating. Human life is indeed full of miraculous love, sensation and wonder.

How can we think of ourselves as existing in the mind of God? What can we say about our lives before we were born? Words may fail us in the face of such a profound mystery.

All we can say is we are each the manifestation of God's infinite divine Love, eternally planned for all time, and joyfully welcomed into existence by our all-knowing Father.

None of us is an accident, for God does not make mistakes. We are individually wanted and desperately loved for all time by the great Life-Giver.

Knowing this makes our lives infinitely more precious, beautiful and meaningful.

A man who authored a book about his vision of heaven wrote that unborn children looked like little lights which appeared to be inhaled and exhaled by God.

Can you imagine that?

Husband discovers new love for wife

Recently a married friend of mine said; "You know, I've discovered that I enjoy being a great husband more than having a great wife."

Puzzled, I asked, "What do you mean?"

"Well," he continued with a wink, "I used to think the best part of marriage was being with an attractive woman. You know, having a trophy wife like mine."

"I still think she's beautiful. But I've come to realize that I find more pleasure in doing special things for her and taking care of her."

He smiled as he spoke, and his eyes gleamed.

"She's been sick for three years now, and I've learned that I like being able to help her. I actually enjoy being the one who is there for her every day to meet her needs, even when she doesn't realize it or appreciate it."

He concluded, "I'm not bragging or anything, it's just true. I've discovered a much deeper love for her and an amazing new outlook on life."

I marveled at his discovery. Here was a grown man being born anew, in full view. In discovering that marriage is about more than his sexual pleasure or raising a family, he was being transformed by the love of God into a new creation.

This is love in the flesh, love personified. The re-birth and re-incarnation of Christ was happening in him.

Here, in the body and mind of my friend, was a new awakening, a new beginning.

This is love God's way, "agape" love, in which the lover seeks only what is best for his beloved.

This is the passionate love of Jesus, totally self-giving. We both lose and find ourselves in it. It overflows in us.

We find this love easily when we seek it with all our heart. And once we discover it, we joyfully sell everything to possess it. (Matthew 13:44)

Those who find this love are truly blessed, and they in turn bless everyone around them.

Whoever finds this love is radically transformed; like the weary traveler who climbs the mountain and gasps at the sight of the Promised Land, or the sinner who stumbles into the cathedral and is astonished by the majesty inside. We discover a love more wonderful than we can imagine.

The man who loves this way is a great warrior. He is superior than any general who conquers a city, for he has conquered himself. (Proverbs 16:32)

In my friend, we can see the reflection of Christ, who sacrificed himself for the sake of his bride, the church. As St. Paul says, "Husbands, love your wives, as Christ loved the Church." (Ephesians 5:25)

This man is a holy man to his wife, for he is devoted to her. His life is consecrated as a result, and it sets him apart from the world and from other women. He has given himself to her alone.

How many women yearn for a lover like this? How many wives would gladly yield to a husband who loves them so completely?

By giving himself entirely to his bride, he sanctifies her and redeems himself. (In return, she may, or may not, give herself completely to him.)

He reveals a deeper dimension of marriage, which is to glorify God and to help each other get to heaven. This love is perfect, and reminds us that we can indeed strive to "be perfect, therefore, as your heavenly father is perfect." (Matthew 5:48)

"This is a profound mystery," says St. Paul, "I am talking about Christ and the Church." (Ephesians 5:32)

When a man loves his wife like this, he loves her the way Jesus loves us.

REJOICING

"This is the day
which the Lord has made;
Let us rejoice and be glad in it."

- Psalm 118

†

Where to see the face of God

I asked my fourth grade class if they thought it was hard to see the face of God.

One boy replied, "It's easy, because God is everywhere."

I congratulated him for his insight and informed him that he might have a future as a great philosopher.

Certainly our Lord wants us to find him. After all, he created us in love. Like an earthly father, our heavenly Father smiles upon us. He wants to gather us together to share his love as a family.

Wait a minute, you say, no one can see God.

Yet we know that "God created man in his image; in the Divine image he created him; male and female he created them." (Genesis 1:27)

Does this mean we look like God? Yes indeed. We all represent the image of our Creator, just as we resemble our earthly parents. Therefore, in some strange and unfathomable way, we can look at any person on the planet and see God.

We may see the face of God clearly in a newborn child or devoted parent, a loving spouse or dear friend.

If we look more closely, we may glimpse the face of God in the smile of a neighbor or teacher, priest or nun, friend or stranger.

If we are pure of heart, Jesus said, we shall see God.

With practice, we see the face of God more often; in a poem, a sonogram or a symphony.

Soon we see God in all that is beautiful -- a reflecting pond, a tail-wagging dog, a snoozing cat, a splendid sunrise, a starry night.

Inevitably something or someone hurts us, and then we sometimes lose sight of the face of God.

Suddenly God seems to just vanish from sight.

Gone is his comforting countenance that gave us hope, light, and life. Instead, we confront the glaring scowls of anger, fear, greed, lust and pride. We recoil from these wicked apparitions, and doubt the goodness of a God who allows such horrors.

Then, if we allow it, the mighty face of God reappears and gives us the wisdom and courage to understand that these terrors are only harmless Halloween-like masks worn by our ancient enemy, Satan; the defiant one who seeks to deceive us and deny our true vision of the goodness of God.

We must look deeper beneath the appearances of life. We will then discover the face of God not only in beauty and celebration, but also hidden underneath the pain and suffering of a fallen and beloved world.

We open our eyes and gaze upon the tear-stained face of God in a hospital bed, a divorce court, or a prison cell.

When at last we behold the face of God disfigured on the cross, bruised by sin, and disguised in death, our vision is nearly complete.

Now with eyes of faith we discern the face of God in everyone, just as we recognize ourselves in a broken mirror, and we reach out with joy to help a suffering world. Then we delight in feeding a hungry mouth, forgiving an unkind word, cooling a fevered brow, and wiping away a sorrowful tear.

Seeing the face of God will always changes us, if we allow ourselves to be transformed in his image. It brings us closer to him, each other, and our salvation.

One day soon we shall behold the wonderful face of God clearly in a beatific vision, then "we shall see him as he is" and "we shall be like him." (1 John 3:2)

Be the radiant face of God to someone today. Let people glimpse in your face a unique and comforting reflection of the Creator of the Universe.

Be more perfect despite your flaws

At my nephew's birthday party, I asked him, "How does it feel to be six years old?"

He thought for a moment, and then with a big smile, he announced, "More perfect!"

What a wonderful sentiment to remind us that we can experience improvement at any age.

We all hope that every day we are getting better and better. Throughout history, people have always sought the elusive Fountain of Youth.

In some ways, of course, we do get better. Especially when we are young we feel ourselves growing stronger, taller, and smarter.

Alas, we need not live very long before we begin to notice our imperfections. Childhood playmates gleefully point out our limitations. We cringe to remember how a schoolmate laughed at us or made a cruel remark about the way we looked, walked or spoke.

A hurtful comment delivered by someone can cut like a knife, reminding us of our faults sometimes years after the insult.

Every glance in the mirror can remind us of our flaws. We notice with dismay that we are too skinny here, too heavy there. Something about our nose, eyes or hair deprives us of looking like our favorite movie star.

As time passes, life conspires to remind us of our shortcomings.

We may be discouraged by a work review, a doctor's diagnosis, or aches and pains that slow us down.

For some of us, poor performance in sports or business lowers our self-esteem. For others, an unfaithful spouse or rebellious child may wrongly incriminate us and imply that we are not who we wish to be.

Despite our best intentions, we may acquire unhealthy ways of thinking, eating or behaving.

A muddled mind or broken heart may lead us to make poor choices. As a result, we can sometimes fall into depression or stumble into harmful addictions.

In many ways, we realize that we are not getting better every day, rather we are getting worse.

At some point, we must begin to accept that we are all subject to a fallen nature.

Then, just when the gathering thunderclouds seem most ominous, the brilliant light of Christ pierces our darkness with a blazing shaft of dazzling sunlight.

"I am the resurrection and the life" Jesus proclaims, "whoever believes in me, even if he dies, will live" (John 11:26).

This is wonderfully good news, informing us "our inner self is being renewed day by day" (2 Cor. 4:16).

To our surprise, Jesus invites and empowers us to achieve this desire; "Be perfect, just as your heavenly Father is perfect" (Matthew 5:48).

This is an impossible dream, we think, but Jesus calls us by name and says, "Follow me" (Matthew 19:21).

Walking in his footsteps, we begin to see that our image in the mirror is a façade. As we look deeper, past appearances, we perceive what is real in ourselves and in others.

Slowly but surely, we understand the Creator's plan. His Son has gone before us to show us the way. He parts the veil of death to reveal our path to paradise, beginning here and now on earth.

His power makes us perfect in spite of our flaws, allowing us to share his resurrection and eternal life.

He renews us every day, moment-by-moment, heartbeat by heartbeat.

As we quietly breathe God's inspiring breath, we discover his loving desire to redeem us; "Whoever is in Christ is a new creation; the old things have passed away; behold, new things have come" (2 Cor. 5:17).

My nephew was right; we really can become "more perfect" every day. That gives me great joy and hope.

†

Moving to a
happy new place

Once upon a time I lived in an out-of-the way place, in a neighborhood called Resentment.

It was a real eyesore, a godforsaken ghetto, with trash strewn everywhere, cars honking, shoppers elbowing, televisions blaring.

The weather was miserable too. Ask anyone, it was always too hot or cold, too rainy or humid, dark and gloomy even at mid-day.

The food and water were awful too, leaving me forever feeling hungry or thirsty.

The people were the worst - so selfish! Everybody was out for themselves. All the business people were hell-bent for money, the politicians were crooked, and the churchgoers were hypocrites. I swear there was something wrong with everyone. I am serious; I could point to every person and tell you exactly what was wrong with him or her and the way s/he irritated me.

But did they listen to me? No way. Their endless chattering was enough to drive anyone to smoke and drink. Nobody cared about me, and no one noticed my problems, at least not to the degree they should have.

So I avoided them, and that suited me just fine. I had my own aches and pains to concern me. It was lonely and depressing, living in such a God-forsaken ghost town.

I could go on forever with my grievances, but you get the picture.

Then I heard about a nearby community called Gratitude. The place sounded too good to be true, and I forgot about it.

Years passed. One day, wanting to get away from all the people who annoyed me in Resentment, I took a walk far from my house. When I entered a nearby community I saw a woman watering her garden with a hose. We got to talking, and after I complained about my neighborhood to her, she told me about her neighborhood. "It's a place called Gratitude" she said, "you'd enjoy living there, too!"

That night I fell into a deep sleep and had a nightmare.

I dreamed I was trying to climb out of a bottomless hole, through tangled thorns that tore at my shirt and skin.

I awoke abruptly at sunrise, and took a ragged breath. I arose and rushed out the door to journey back to Gratitude.

Everything there looked familiar, yet somehow different.

A paperboy rode by and threw me the morning edition, shouting "Good News!"

I strolled down the street and met an old woman at the curb. I offered my arm to help her across. She said "Thank you" and smiled. "You're welcome," I replied. Then I noticed a strange sensation: I felt as though I was walking on air.

I approached three men to ask directions. They waved and called to me. "Join us for some exercise," one exclaimed. "Good for the heart, you know, reaching down and lifting people up!" I replied, "Yes; later, thanks!" and felt happier than I had in a long time.

I passed a playground filled with laughing children, and found myself mingling with all their parents, teachers, and coaches. Their eyes sparkled like stained-glass windows lit by the rising sun.

Well, it took me awhile but one day I finally up and moved from Resentment to that wonderful neighborhood called Gratitude. Now I am delighted to be living here. I tell my new neighbors every day how glad I am to be their fellow citizen.

People say the beauty here is thanks to our Governor, a benevolent old man with white hair who obviously keeps things running smoothly. He is somewhat mysterious, so I do not know much about him. Everyone calls him "Abba", and he hosts a candlelight supper every week at his house, serving tasty bread and fine wine. He authored a bestselling book that I intend to read sometime. I will get around to it one of these days.

In the meantime, I am happy I moved to Gratitude.

You are made new in God's garden of life

In my garden a clay tablet reads, "A kiss of the sun for pardon, the song of the birds for mirth, one is nearer God's heart in a garden, than anywhere else on earth."

Each spring I feel a sense of wonder as I plant in my secluded oasis.

I enjoy turning the moist ground with my shovel, preparing it to receive the seeds of new life.

In my pockets I carry my favorite seeds; including tomatoes, corn, peas, watermelons, cantaloupes and cucumbers.

I delight in each of their special shapes and qualities.

Some prefer dry soil; others do better in wet soil. Some require full sun; others favor shade.

From experience, I know each of their unique requirements, so I carefully plant each seed in exactly the right spot in the garden.

One by one, I take each seed and push it deep into the sweet, fragrant earth with my finger. Next, I cover every one with fine, organic topsoil.

As I work, drops of salty sweat appear on my brow and fall silently onto the thirsty earth.

Finally, with my water hose I soak the furrows and beds.

Now I wait in joyful anticipation. A miracle is in the making.

Sure enough, a few days later, little green sprouts magically pop up and reach toward the sun. Each new plant is a bountiful sign of the mystery of creation and the renewal of life. Soon my family will rejoice in an abundant harvest.

I am participating in the mystery of creation, co-operating with God and renewing the face of the earth. This was the first job God gave to Adam; to take care of the Garden of Eden.

As I work in my garden in the cool of the day, I hear God's voice in the whispering breeze, the fluttering leaves, and buzzing bumblebees. All creation sings his name, and his imprint is everywhere apparent.

God knows exactly where to plant us and he carefully chooses the perfect place.

As seeds, we only know that we find ourselves suddenly pushed down into darkness.

Naturally, we feel fearful and alone. In our distress, we wonder why God abandons us this way. Doesn't he care that we are buried alive, we are suffocating, that we cannot move or see? We are anxious about our future, and we fear dying.

It is during this uneasy time that we should rest in the comfort our Lord gives to each of us.

Jesus says, "Amen, amen, I say to you, unless a grain of wheat falls to the ground and dies, it remains just a grain of wheat; but if it dies, it produces much fruit" (John 12:24).

Christ invites us to die to our selfishness so that he may liberate his Divine life hidden within us.

He calls us to let go of anger, greed and pride. As we die to our sinful vices, we are reborn in virtuous life.

In what way are you called to die to yourself today? Jesus promises to walk with you, watch over you, and guide you.

We may rejoice that our hard shells are cracking, sprouting new life, and gracefully rising toward the Son.

Soon we will hardly recognize ourselves, so lushly fertile and bountiful will we be. Such profusion, such generosity, such beauty!

Our new life will be unimaginably more fertile than the life we now live, producing the fruits and seeds of an ever-increasing harvest and surpassing our comprehension.

This is our life in Christ, bursting forth in endless abundance, lovingly cultivated by the mighty hand of God.

I know God is the Master Gardener, and we are his seeds.

He knows each one of us better than we know ourselves.

†
God lives in
a special place

One day my 4-year old nephew began peppering his mother with questions about God.

"Is God married?" he asked. "Is God invisible? Does God give everyone candy?"

His mother tried to answer his questions to the best of her ability.

A few weeks later, as they drove to church on Sunday, the mystery behind his curiosity was apparently solved. As they drove past the rectory he pointed and declared, "That's where God lives."

After Mass, she related this funny story to our parish priest, informing him that he had been promoted.

When we are young children, most of us assume grown-ups are god-like because they appear powerful and super-sized to a pint-sized kid.

Priests appear especially god-like to children. In a way this is right, because priests have answered a call from God to consecrate themselves, to set themselves apart in order to "be Christ" to his people on earth.

Priests are ordained to celebrate the Sacraments "in persona Christi", a Latin phrase meaning "in the person of Christ".

In other words, Christ acts through the priest in the Sacraments. This is a God-given gift bestowed by Jesus originally on his disciples.

In a similar way, all married men are called to be priests to their wives; "Husbands, love your wives, just as Christ loved the church and gave himself up for her" (Ephesians 5:25).

Thus, when a husband loves his wife, we may say of him "God lives there."

Nuns are also called to let Christ occupy and guide their lives. In a special way, nuns are spiritual brides of Christ and mothers of God, re-presenting him to the world

In reality, all people are called to be priestly and Christ-like. As Saint Peter said, "You are a chosen people, a royal priesthood" (1 Peter 2:9).

Everyone is created to receive God's royal love and to let him dwell in us. It is our choice whether or not we accept this love and let him in.

From the moment of our conception, God provides in us the spark of his divine essence and inspires us with his holy breath of life. Surely our Creator smiles at us and thinks; "That's where I live."

We receive Christ physically into our bodies whenever we receive the Eucharist. Therefore, when we see people returning from Communion we may indeed think, "God lives there."

Jesus invites us to receive God in another intimate and mysterious way: "I will ask the Father, and he will give you another Counselor to be with you forever; the Spirit of truth... you know him, for he lives with you and will be in you" (John 14:15). Thus we are living, breathing temples of the Holy Spirit and share in the life of the Trinity.

As we grow in faith, we realize that God inhabits all of us and clothes us with new life. We come to understand God indwells his entire creation, except where there is sin.

Sadly, we may minimize God's life within us with selfish thoughts, words and deeds.

Happily, though, when we obey his will in love, Christ promises to live in each one of us; "I am in my Father, and you are in me, and I am in you" (John 14:20).

This is a marvelous miracle to contemplate: God lives in me, and I live in God.

We can become so filled with the love of God that we may say with Paul, "It is no longer I who live, but Christ who lives in me" (Galatians 2:20).

Then everyone who meets us may later say with delight, "That's where God lives."

To find joy, give it away

Once a rich farmer saw some poor people in his village, and he was moved to tears.

So he gave his son a one hundred dollar bill and said, "Son, I want you to take this money and give it to someone in need."

The boy ran into town, looked around and spotted a poor man sitting on the curb.

He stuffed the one hundred dollar bill into the man's dirty hands.

Surprised, the poor man immediately ran into the food store and purchased one hundred dollars' worth of food from the grocer.

Delighted, the grocer ran to pay his debt of one hundred dollars to the butcher.

Eagerly, the butcher ran to pay his debt of one hundred dollars to the baker.

Thankfully, the baker ran to pay his debt of one hundred dollars to the candlestick maker.

Gratefully, the candlestick maker ran to pay his debt of one hundred dollars to the grocer.

The grocer then ran to the boy's house and knocked on his door.

When the boy opened the door, the grocer handed him the one hundred dollar bill and exclaimed, "Thank you, your generosity has paid everyone's debts! The whole town now looks to the future with optimism. Here is your one hundred dollar bill with my gratitude."

The boy ran joyfully to his father to return the money.

His father said, "Well done, my son."

This old-fashioned story shows what each of us can do with a dollar, a smile, or a kind word.

Whenever you give someone something, it is like tossing a pebble into a pond - the ripples spread outward until they cover the entire pond.

Try it today and remember, "One man gives freely, yet gains even more" (Proverbs 11:24). The next person you meet, pay him a sincere compliment or say an encouraging word. Watch as your words bring a smile to his face and brighten his day.

Imagine him, inspired by you, giving a similar compliment to another person, and so on.

Your one compliment may multiply endlessly.

Scientists describe a phenomenon known as "The Butterfly Effect". The idea that one butterfly could eventually have a far-reaching ripple effect on subsequent events was made famous by meteorologist Edward Lorenz, who said that one flap of a butterfly's wings could change the course of weather forever. When a butterfly flaps its wings, it creates tiny changes in the atmosphere that may ultimately cause a tornado or a hurricane on the other side of the planet.

If one flap of a butterfly's wings can change the weather on the other side of the earth, imagine what you can do with a kind deed or an uplifting word!

Let us be generous and spread our blessings around. Give your gifts freely to others and watch them multiply.

We cannot know the extent of our influence, especially when we allow God to work through us. When we cooperate with God, even the smallest things we do may cause big changes in others.

You may be happy and healthy or sad and uncertain about your future, but you can still toss a pebble of joy into the sea of life.

Your Creator is waiting to help, so as you pray the Lord's Prayer, stand by and let the mighty power of God work through you. Let him use you to help change the world.

Jesus said, "A farmer went out to sow his seed...it came up and yielded a crop, a hundred times more than was sown" (Luke 8:5).

✝
My Notes of Joyful Praise

✝

My Notes of Joyful Praise

✝

My Notes of Joyful Praise

✝
My Notes of Joyful Praise

✝
My Notes of Joyful Praise

✝

My Notes of Joyful Praise

✝
My Notes of Joyful Praise

✝
My Notes of Joyful Praise

✝
My Notes of Joyful Praise